HOMESPUN

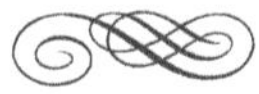

TRUE TALES OF TWEED

J. JOSEPH PASTRANA

THANE&PROSE

Thane & Prose, New York

Published by Thane & Prose, 495 Henry Street, Brooklyn, NY 11231

First Printing, 2022

ISBN 978-0-578-35020-2

PRINTED IN THE UNITED STATES OF AMERICA

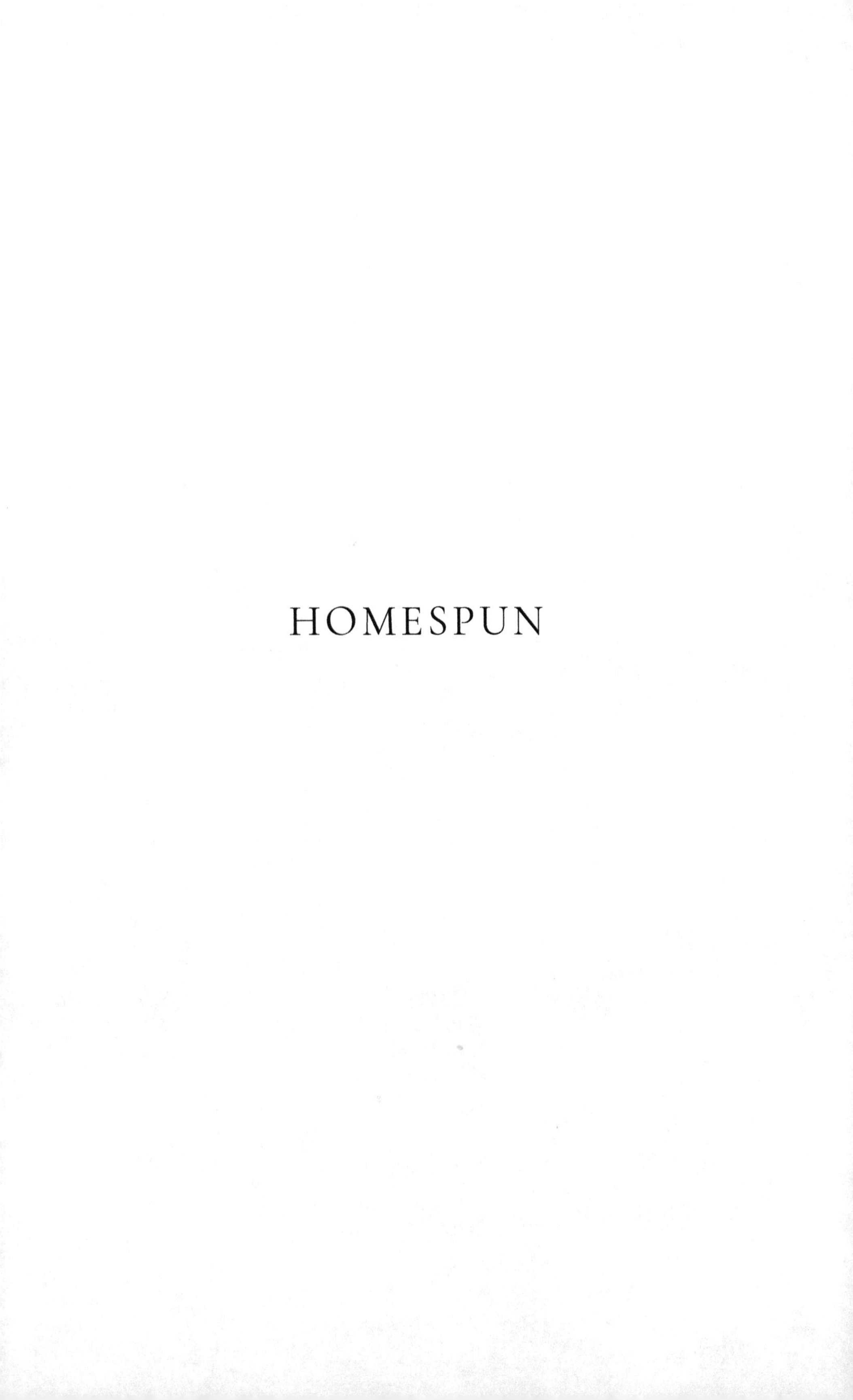

HOMESPUN

Contents

Dedication

For my grandmother,
my father,
and New York City,
from whom and where all my notions of home were spun

I

The Stuff That Dreams Are Made Of

Everyone on the F train was going to think he was crazy. And, he was going to be late for his own wedding. Those were the frantic thoughts of Will Burghes as he dashed into a subway car wearing full morning tails one Summer morning in 2012. But summoning conveyance with a swipe on a phone app was still years away and he had already spent what seemed like an eternity in desperate search for a cab. He knew his fate now depended entirely on the capricious whims of the MTA gods.

As the train rattled loudly down the subterranean tunnels of New York City, he felt the sheen of anxious sweat spread uncontrollably on his skin. And aggravated by the stranglehold of heat, it began seeping through his once pristine white shirt. With the vehicle lurching precipitously toward its destination, Will steadied his footing and began taking off his morning coat. He carefully draped it across an arm and, with his free hand, hung onto an overhead rail. Stealing quick glances around, he realized his earlier concern had been totally unfounded. To these seen-it-all straphangers, there was nothing at all unusual about a 6-foot-five Englishman, impeccably garbed in a dress shirt, wool waistcoat, gray striped trousers, and Balmoral boots on his sweaty way to his nuptials. In fact, Will belatedly noticed how, among the variedly dressed passengers there, he hardly ranked among those worth a second glance. All the same, he had no regrets over his wedding attire. He was marrying the most fascinating woman he had ever met today. And he was as determined to seal the deal in garb that would properly express not just the certitude and depth of his feelings but the seriousness with which he viewed the ceremony. Five years later, he would take a similarly well-considered plunge when he decided that he would at last fulfill another one of his dreams. Will was going to commission a tweed suit.

- - - - - - -

Tweed has always captivated Will Burghes. His determination to have a suit made out of this singular cloth may be dismissed by some as a trifling indulgence. Others may summarily deride tweed as merely a sentimental memento from a bygone era, something best left in a romanticized haze of nostalgia. And yet, they would be wrong. Because tweed is infinitely more than all that. Within its myriad weaves are tales of fortitude and grace intricately entwined with the lives and livelihoods of countless people across centuries and several continents. From humble beginnings to the heights of prestige and glamour, tweed's history is threaded by hope, success, and heartbreaking reversals of fortune.

But does tweed still matter to this social media-addicted generation? Why does it continue to exert a hold on the imagination of the world's most creative designers? And how can it still inspire them in conceiving fresh interpretations and new applications?

Perhaps in a not entirely surprising turn, as everyone becomes ever more tethered to digital devices, people are actually rediscovering and appreciating all things analog. While most major corporations double down on hawking deliberately transitory products, a growing number of consumers are seeking their antitheses. Witness the rush to find the next "artisanal" obsession, or the resurgence of vinyl records. Certainly, there will always be those for whom reliving the past is an enticing idea. Then there are some who may simply be interested in boarding the next departing bandwagon. Nonetheless, tweed has weathered decades of inexorable cultural and social progress, technological advancements, and vacillating tastes to remain a formidable presence in fashion and related industries. In the warmth and comfort of wearing tweed is pride in the past, sophistication in the present, and indeed dreams of a better future.

To truly understand tweed, however, one must begin at its ancestral home in the northernmost country of the United Kingdom. Over the years, the volume of ink spilled in efforts to satisfactorily commit Scotland to poetry and song should by now be enough to fill a loch. Epic sagas of heroism and tragedy, resilience and determination have been recorded throughout Norse invasions, skirmishes with the British Empire, periods of famine, and internecine clashes among the lairds. Yet, all those breathless accounts still fall short of fully explaining the land's near mystical aura, the indescribable enchantment that befall anyone who sees its panoramas for the first time. Only such a magical place could have complected tweed into being. No other fabric has a constitution woven from out of haunting scenery, rugged terrain, and an intemperate climate. Its sheep provides the wool, its flora the dyes, and its melancholic beauty the allure that continues to captivate millions.

The very origin of the word "tweed" is mired in unresolved contention. The most widely held story is the one that lays blame on shoddy penmanship. In 1826, Wm. Watson & Sons of Dangerfield Mills in Hawick is said to have sent a shipment of twills or "tweels" to one Mr. James Locke, a London merchant on 119 Regent Street, London. The invoice was allegedly misread by a clerk or Locke himself, either of whom thereafter re-ordered further supplies referring to them as "tweeds". It's a charming anecdote that alas doesn't hold up because Locke was a known purveyor of Scottish woolens. He is even claimed to have been instrumental in making the fabrics popular in London. There simply would have been no basis for this sort of misunderstanding. Others believe the word is in reference to the River Tweed, which flows east along the borders of Scotland and Northern England, the environs of which the cloth is thought to have been conceived. The least romantic, and arguably the most probable, is tweed was simply a truncated way of referring to material that's been "tweeled". Whichever account may or may not be true, trade documentation from the 1830s-1840s confirms use of the term. And tweed it's been called ever since.

Technically, twill is the weaving technique characterized by passing the weft (the horizontal threads) over the warp (longitudinal threads) and then under two or more warp threads to result in a diagonal rib pattern on the finished fabric. Because the right side of the twill is unevenly textured, it is found to ably resist stains and dirt. In cotton, the most common twill is denim. There are actually many kinds of weaving patterns that can be used on natural or synthetic yarn and still be called "twill fabric". These include checked, houndstooth, chevron, bird's eye, diamond, and herringbone (a typical twill pattern so named because it looks like the skeletal structure of the herring fish). Depending on the thickness of the yarn, the pattern can be less or more visible as opposed to the simpler "over and under" plain weave method that results in a relatively leveled surface.

Tweed is a woolen twill fabric that first found use for the making of humble yet hardy garments of country folk, of farmers and fishermen who needed sturdy everyday clothing that could withstand the harsh elements. It would come to be celebrated for intrinsic qualities that have endured despite and maybe even because of its many incarnations. It is a cloth of tactile substance, tensile strength, and visual depth. Its construct plays with light and shadow, and catches air and water. The patterns and colors may carry meaning or provoke an emotional kind of Rorschachian reading in their seemingly aleatory arrangements. Forever stationed in some liminal space, it is undeniably heritage while appearing confoundingly modern.

The traditional way of making tweed involved first mordanting the wool in salt, coloring, then "carding" (the sorting and cleaning of the fibers), spinning, and finally weaving a "plaiding" or blanket. Spinning wool into yarn was primitively done entirely by hand, wrapping the flax around a distaff while operating a spindle. When the spinning wheel (believed to have originated from the Islamic regions in the 10th century) became more widely available, it allowed the operator to keep the spindle in motion by pedaling on a treadle instead of using hands. These were so popular in the Highlands one could say they were the antiquated equivalent of the toaster as the common wedding present to Scottish brides. And for generations throughout Scotland and Ireland, the custom of making garments and fabrics at home for personal use was so until demand for woolen goods led to a cottage industry that spread to other regions. As a means of making a living, it became more lucrative than fishing, and trade would escalate exponentially once rail made transporting people and goods more efficient. Soon Scotland's rural landscape was dotted with industrial towns.

Among the first places to produce woolen goods in commercial quantities was Edinburgh where its weavers were incorporated by the town council as early as 1475. The manufacture and trade of woolen goods continued to expand at pace with advancements in machinery. Weaving by vertical or horizontal loom, known to have been in practice since 700 AD, continued to be a laborious process, undergoing sporadic improvements until the power-loom was introduced to upgrade quality and increase output. Cloth, carpets, and stockings of tartans, checks, and flannels made in Dunbar, Inverness, Linton, Perth, Tranent, Linlithgow, and Glasgow were eventually exported not just to England but across Europe. Broadcloths of finer fibers made in Aberdeenshire came to be accepted as being at par with, if not superior to, those produced from English looms.

Color being a paramount virtue of tweeds made the dyeing process (as well as the quality of the dyes) critical to its production. But because of the era's limitations in the understanding of the chemical properties of dyes, when it came to the colors of different kinds of fabrics few were dependably lasting. Up until the 17th century it was routine for English broadcloth to be sent to dye plants in Holland for that country's more advanced coloring techniques. Also, there weren't many people qualified in dyeing for commercial production, which, in those days, required knowledge in the diverse fields of botany, chemistry, and the arts. Aside from the necessity of understanding the properties of the dyes and their respective color tones, one had to know how to layer dyes in the proper sequence to achieve a certain shade. Then there's the matter of how not all dyes interact effectually with plant fibers as they would with those from an animal. Finally, there's the aforementioned matter of ensuring the color doesn't fade after washing or from direct and prolonged exposure to sunlight.

For tweed, dyeing is implemented not on the finished fabric but on the wool. According to folklore, adding color to wool was precipitated by the early practice of mixing tar and butter then smearing the blend on sheep as a protective layer against the frigid temperatures of the Highlands. The concoction was applied on the skin of the sheep but inevitably stained its wool a heavy shade of cream. This led to affecting other shades by mixing in ragweed, dandelions, heather, along with other flowers and plants as coloring agents. For a time, urine was fermented in barrels and used as the fixative. That practice was later abandoned for chemical dyes which rendered a reliably longer lasting and standardized palette. Wool is steeped in these liquids at boiling temperature to enable the dye to fasten unto the fibers. Once these are spun into yarns, creativity is required in laying out the different colored strands into the best combinations of textured weaves that magnify contrasts as well the interplay of light and shadow for which tweed is unmatched.

- - - - - - -

For Will Burghes, tweed represents more than an arbitrary fabric choice. It is a very tangible link to his own forebears, an indefinable way of staying connected to who he is. By most indications, Will is rather typical of most New Yorkers. At thirtysomething, he lives in Brooklyn with his wife Whitney, and their ten year-old mixed-breed poodle called Shadow. He rides a bicycle to work as executive director of data and analytics at the Manhattan office of multinational creative agency Forsman & Bodenfors. He came from elsewhere, in his case, the United Kingdom. He relocated for a job, when an offer came to join Citigroup.

And as a point of clarification, he isn't unreasonably punctilious about dressing. Closer to the mark may be that Will lies somewhere between a card-carrying acolyte in the fashion cult and someone for whom a pair of jeans is fine for any occasion. It's just that, like countless other opinionated inhabitants of the five boroughs, he knows what he wants to wear. But those indelible preferences were formed back in merry ole England.

Will grew up in the South-West London district of Clapham during the 1990s when it had already lost many palatial homes to demolition and redevelopments. Though it is now a prosperous neighborhood, the Clapham of Will's youth was the everyman's commuter suburb of modest repute. In the working class neighborhood, the seeds were sown in his upbringing to root in Will a respect for wearing clothes appropriate for the occasion. An important presence in his early years was his maternal grandfather, Ronnie Burghes who passed away in 1997. The older Mr. Burghes and his wife, Will's grandmother, who was a photographer, resided in nearby Fulham where Will, his parents, and his younger brother John would routinely spend Friday night dinners.

As a young man, Will's grandfather volunteered in the Spanish Civil War and fought during the second world war. "During the war, he was shot in the chest and the bullet went right through him. My grandmother was mistakenly informed that my grandfather had died because they didn't find him until a day or so after," Will recounts. "But the bullet did leave a scar." And apparently more than a physical one because along with it came a reticence about any talk of the war. The veteran was determined not to relive a time he equated to senseless suffering. Like all British men of his generation with a military background, his way of dressing was marked by habitual regimentation. "We have many pictures of him still hanging on our walls at home. And in every photo of him, whether in his military uniforms or 'civvies', he was always correctly attired," says Will. Those photographs were constant reminders of how a man he loved and admired comported himself and Will would take it all to heart. He can still imagine his grandfather's preferences, "Tweed or a shetland sweater would have been his idea of activewear for a hike. And because he was also half Scottish, he and my grandmother loved shopping for tartan at the Scotch House (the woolen and cashmere shop in London that closed in 2001)."

By example and instruction however, the most influential figure in Will's life was his father Stephen Powell. They shared several interests that developed into predilections Will still has to this day. An avid cycler, Will recalls his father teaching him how to ride a bike. "And, we'd ride our own bicycles together every morning on the way to elementary school where I would be dropped off and he'd go on to bike to his work." They also shared an avocation for photography. "My father always had a camera hanging around his neck," he notes. And like cycling, Will continues to take amateur photos of landscapes and architecture. But perhaps most pertinently, Powell taught Will the fundamentals of how to dress. Powell, an economist, started wearing business suits daily when adherence to a professional appearance held graver consequences than they might today. Many were the stories Will heard his father tell him dealing with the implicit codes of work dressing.

Will remembers Powell talking to him about a friend who had been promoted to partner at the London law firm Slaughter & May. One hot summer day, this man entered the partners' dining room and after sitting down realized that a hush had suddenly descended around him. Confused, he looked around and found everyone pointedly staring at the most senior partner present, who then stood up and approached his father's friend. The senior partner leaned over and in a hushed tone suggested that despite the heat, he might feel more comfortable with his jacket on. According to Will, "It seems that my father's friend had unconsciously taken it off due to the warmth, momentarily forgetting that while in the dining room, it was a breach of etiquette not to be wearing a jacket."

In another incident, when Powell was employed in a bank, he was walking down a hallway alongside a colleague who had on a grey herringbone jacket when they were stopped by one of the company partners. "The partner said to my father's co-worker 'Going to the races?'" It was an off-hand remark that was no less effective in very strongly suggesting for Powell's colleague to go home and change into something less casual and more in line with the work environment. "My father really impressed upon me the importance of dressing to the context of an occasion." Will muses, "It probably says something that when he retired, he bought himself a magnificent tweed suit. Though I'm not sure if he still has it."

Adapting a more relaxed business attire toward the end of the work week has its antecedents, predictably enough, in the US. It was in the mid 1960s when the Hawaiian Fashion Guild gifted all the members of the state's House of Representatives and the Hawaiian Senate with two Hawaiian shirts each, by way of proposing that civil service employees be allowed to wear lightweight garments during the summer (and incidentally feel motivated to buy more Hawaiian shirts). A decade later, this had become a routine referred to as "Aloha Friday", which of course became Casual Friday for the rest of the US. Similarly, in London, while formal business attire was mandated Mondays through Thursdays, segments of the civil service were in due course allowed to wear tweed on Fridays. "This was on the misguided assumption that everyone would be retreating to the country at the end of the work week," Will points out, "despite how very few civil servants were likely to have had country homes."

It's worth noting that these incidents were merely a couple of generations ago. So culturally embedded were many of these unwritten rules of business attire that to Will's recollection divergences from these occurred only recently. He notes, "Up until around the Big Bang (the term used in reference to Margaret Thatcher's 1986 abrupt deregulation of financial markets), many finance jobs in London more or less still required wearing bowler hats, while stroller suits or cutaways were expected in other professions." It may surprise most Americans how many businesses in the UK still comply (consciously or otherwise) to the old "no brown in town" edict. The phrase, believed to have arisen in the 1930s, pertains to how one only wears brown and green (tweeds) in the country (during the weekends), while blue suits and black shoes are preferred in town (or the city).

As late as 2019, a Twitter storm erupted when someone mentioned that during a London Thomson Reuters conference, an unnamed partner at a law firm was overheard reminding his subordinates not to wear brown shoes with their blue suits. While opposing sides vigorously thumbed their 140-character arguments, studies showed that during job interviews, brown shoes still won't get a candidate past the front door. And if the job opening happens to be at a company with the eminence of say Lloyd's of London, woe betide an applicant without a pair of black Oxford Cheaneys.

In 1991, Will attended Dulwich College (Est. 1619), the boarding school for boys where it was and still is mandatory to wear a uniform. Will recalls, "The school uniform was somewhat formal, consisting of a black single-breasted jacket over a white shirt, fastened at the collar and tucked into a pair of charcoal grey trousers, an approved college tie (of which there were many variations, depending on the teams and clubs one belonged to, and the awards or status that had been granted by the school), plain dark gray or black socks and plain black polished leather shoes." Should it be necessary to don a coat, the rules explicitly say it would have to be one of "sober hue and cut" with plain buttons and no insignia; while scarves must be in college colors. Pride still rings when Will talks of Dulwich, which has long held a very progressive reputation of inclusiveness when it came to race, class, or economic status. "But, you had to earn the privilege of being able to wear a jacket with the school's cornflower blue stripes by some accomplished academic or athletic merit," he explains, securing his when he became Dulwich's crew captain in 1997.

"I spent a couple of years participating at various regattas held in the country," he says. Some of those attracted the similarly well-dressed crowds that flock to the annual Henley Royal or Marlow Regatta. "The spectators in attendance, regardless if they had ever been rowers themselves, would mostly be wearing striped boating blazers, suits and tweeds." But at this stage, Will was for the most part oblivious to what he wore when he was out of school uniform. He admits, "I was not particularly interested in clothes when I was young. Like every one of my friends, I went to a lot of concerts and mostly wore band T-shirts, jeans, hooded sweaters, trainers, and so forth."

In 2003, Will earned a degree in Economics and Philosophy from the University of Bristol (Est. 1876); and a year later received his masters from the London School of Economics and Political Science (Est. 1895). His carefree attitude with regards to clothes pivoted sharply once he started working at Oliver Wyman, the management consultancy firm focused on the finance industry. He was reminded of his father's stories and diligently observed all the customs of dressing for work in the new millennium. It was still invariably business suit and tie when meeting with clients. And although business casual on average work days had become acceptable, the line on the corporate floor was still indelibly drawn against jeans. Will thrived in the world of finance. He says, "The company itself had a great atmosphere and staffed with smart people. The work involved generally long hours but challenging and rewarding, with lots of travel to pretty interesting and fun cities within Europe, but also the Middle East and the US." One American city, however, would keep pulling at Will. And like moth to the incandescent glow of the New York skyline, he came.

"I first visited New York in 2000 to see old friends and I kept coming back every year," he says. "I had no money so I would just explore the different neighborhoods and there was always something new to discover. I don't know when I began to seriously think I would want to live here but I did," he confides. "When a friend told me about a job opening in New York, I saw it as a rare opportunity to make it happen." The job was as vice president of markets and investment banking strategy for Citibank. It was definitely an important career advancement but it wasn't without some hand-wringing. "I was excited, yes, but I also had to leave everything, my home, my family and friends." Any misgivings were quickly overcome by his certainty that such an opportunity may not come again.

He arrived in October 2008. And like so many others before him, he decided to move into the legendary capital of downtown bohemian lifestyle, the West Village. This was when rents were still bound by some semblance of sanity. But, he laughs, "I ended up in this nasty, mice-in-fested, one bedroom apartment walk up. The walls were so thin you could hear everything in the building, from people walking down the halls to whatever was going on next door. For the entire year I lived there, I heard my neighbors snoring in their sleep." But probably more disturbing than his living situation was learning that the promising new chapter in his career may have been doomed to fail. Will says that his hiring happened to coincide with what was also "up until then perhaps the worst month that the financial industry had seen in my lifetime. It was not long after the bankruptcy of Lehman Brothers. There were too many unemployed finance people and scant job openings. The indus-try was suffused by so much uncertainty." He deadpans, "It was not an auspicious start." Will was relieved that somehow though he managed to keep his job; and the financial sector settled once more. And fortu-nately as well, he was able to later move to a quieter apartment, and one presumably free of vermin.

New York also began to impose on Will the kind of sociological sway that affects everyone who lives here. Most Americans prefer to believe their agency is based solely on internal motivations, perhaps unaware of how their behavior adjusts to norms and incentives endemic in institu-tional settings. The writer Upton Sinclair (1878-1968) documented his ill-fated run for Governor of California in his 1935 book "I, Candidate for Governor: And How I Got Licked". In it he wrote, "It is difficult to get a man to understand something, when his salary depends upon his not understanding it." Conversely, understanding something becomes paramount when one's salary does depend on it. In dressing, this phe-nomenon can be seen in its sharpest reliefs in Wall Street and the fash-ion industry. When observing how fashion people dress, it is intriguing how both conformity and individuality are concurrently served. If one were employed, for instance, at either Condé Nast or Hearst, the pub-lishing offices of the leading fashion magazines, one would feel natu-rally compelled to dress fashionably. Little wonder the lobbies of these buildings become veritable catwalks at the peak of the morning rush.

And while yes, fashion prizes distinction, that in itself may also be regarded as collectivist thinking.

So while Will adjusted to the way businessmen in New York dressed, he also became consciously aware of the visible discrepancies in how New Yorkers and Londoners dressed. He says, "Early on, everyone seemed starkly informal to my eyes. The doormen at Barclays in London wore frock coats. In New York, even five star hotel doormen just wore grey suits." At American formal settings, he observed more pronounced details that would be verboten in the UK. "Jacket cuts were roomier. I noticed a lot of button down collars, breast pockets, and striped ties. British men only own and wear striped ties that represent their school, regiment or club." Perhaps most egregious was the presence of tasseled loafers at certain settings. But then one doesn't have to be British to find those unforgivably galling at a formal event. Other things though made better sense to Will. "British summers are not as hot as in New York, so over in London people tend to stick to blues and greys. It was easier to understand tan and light-colored linen suits in New York where some summer days can be unbearably hot. But seersucker, for example, more or less does not exist in the UK."

To some degree these details became part of Will's acclimation to life in the city. "In London, people kept their jackets on in the office. But in New York your suit jacket stayed on the back of your chair all day, from the moment you arrived until you left at night. Still, since I already had a business wardrobe I was well set up for joining the finance community in New York." He adds, "Another thing I observed was how the entire younger generation of bankers dressed almost exclusively in Brooks Brothers. They probably had fathers who shopped for clothes there. I went once but was unimpressed with the quality and fit of the clothes so I never went back. The quality may have dropped between the generations."

Interestingly enough, only a few years later, Will heard how multinational investment bank UBS (Union Bank of Switzerland) had issued a risible 44-page document outlining its dress code to employees. It contained cringe worthy nuggets of wisdom such as "lengthen the life of your stockings or tights (with) well-trimmed and smooth toenails", "avoid offensive odors (such as) breath smelling of garlic or onions (or the) smell of tobacco", and "always choose underwear so that it is functional and is not seen through your outer clothing". Right on cue, mockery from all corners of the globe came fast and furious. The bank was forced to issue a formal defensive response to the effect that while the mandatory dress code for men was still a dark suit, black shoes, white shirt and red tie, the "guide" was only meant to offer recommendations. It would henceforth be revised into a booklet that "will concentrate on how to impress customers with a polished presence and sense of Swiss precision."

While Will felt it important to rely on the long-held rules of business dressing, he also began to appreciate the more diverse and expressive ways New Yorkers wore their clothes. "No one cared how you were dressed walking around," Will said. "You could be dressed in a hot pink suit and would attract only a few second looks compared to the reactions you might get in London." Will likened this to his previous reaction during a visit to Amsterdam fifteen years ago. "In Amsterdam there seems to be an attitude of not being embarrassed about how you lived your life and not judging how other people lived theirs. The curtains of people's homes were often kept open. They had nothing to hide. In that way it is a 'liberal' city in the original sense of the word ~ that people should be able to act how they want as long as it does not impact someone else's life, without fear of anyone telling them what to do." It also occurred to Will that vestiges of New Amsterdam still existed in present day New York. "The city is very closely related to Amsterdam historically, and I wonder if some of that attitude remains. Everyone is doing their own thing and it's their business. It's not your place to judge."

When Will first took that position with Citibank, he thought he would spend a couple of productive yet fun years in New York and return to London. But when Whitney Smith walked into his life, everything changed. They first met through mutual friends for a dinner get together at the downtown seafood restaurant Mermaid Inn. She worked in sustainable building design and the Englishman was instantly besotted. "She was funny, energetic, and beautiful," he uncharacteristically gushes. They would become closer as they continued to meet on group hangouts until one evening when all pretense of friendship dropped with a kiss. The two went on to share several interests including going to concerts headlined by Ben Harper, Leon Bridges, or Trombone Shorty. She soon moved into his apartment and thoughts of leaving New York were forgotten. In 2010, they were in Europe to attend a friend's wedding and decided to spend a day in Paris. On a casual walk over one of the French capital's romantic bridges, Will proposed. By then Will already had the ring for two months. And Whitney's response was never in question. They were married at one of New York's scenic wedding venues, Central Park's Summit Rock on that blistering September day in 2012 when Will had to take the subway to make it there on time. Of course, Will's entire family flew in to share in the joyous day.

As happy as Will was at home, life in finance and all its constitutional bureaucracy began to make his work feel like drudgery. "I couldn't see myself making a long term career within the office culture prevalent in large banks," he confesses. He looked into other fields before finally making the move to the athletic events startup Tough Mudder founded by friend Will Dean. Being in a "fitness"-based workplace provided Will with more reasons to dial back his formal workwear. "Though I still wore suits, I was finally able to let go of ties," he says. "It was a very casual environment. Many people were literally out in the field, all over the country in rural locations working in all weather, and surrounded by mud and dirt. In the office, since most everyone who worked there focused on fitness and sport, a number of employees ran or cycled to work. Some would go on lunch break runs since we had showers at the office." Internal conflict within Tough Mudder however caused Will to change jobs yet again and that's how he ended up at Forsman & Bodenfors.

These days, one can hardly make out the zenith of advertising on a rearview mirror. Thus Forsman & Bodenfors, founded in 1986, is packaged as a "creative" agency. Though still involved in the traditional forms of ad agency work such as media planning and buying, its forte lies in those catchall terms "branding" and "digital activations". At the risk of belaboring the point, sharply suited and immaculately Brylcreemed Mad men taking martini-and-cigarette lunches this was not. Will avers, "Ad agencies have their own codes and rules, which I tend to ignore completely. Lots of industry people wear only black (which also might be more of a New York thing), or they just wear very informal clothing. People on the business side of the agency still dressed slightly more formally; but it was still business casual at best."

Here, the added creative component gave Will further license to dress more adventurously. "Being one of the few English people in the office gives me extra leeway to dress how I want," he admits. Besides, he says "I enjoy trying new things and am not afraid of dressing badly now and then. It's how you learn. Figure out what you like and what works for you in terms of cloth, fit, style etc. It's a journey and no one gets it right immediately, why not just have fun with it?" So he's taken to embracing more colors and larger patterns. "I was thirteen when my height just shot up and ever since then I have always been able to get away with wearing a lot of checks," he says. But what may be wrongly construed as eccentric British affectations are sincere ways for Will to connect with his own heritage and give it outer expression. In reasserting the qualities he felt made him indelibly British, Will finally became a New Yorker.

It was in that regard that Will's interest in the woolen cloth, ever present when he was growing up, increased and led him to constantly look for suits in the city. If he had his way, there would be more second-hand or vintage garment shops in New York. What few there are however, none come anywhere close to the breadth of what London shops like Hornets or The Vintage Showroom offers (or the now sadly closed Old Hat, which had an ardent base of shoppers for its inventory of tweed suits, dinner jackets, and tails). "In general there seems to be fewer options in New York for places to shop for suits that aren't too pricey," he points out. "This is rather a contrast to London where there are dozens of different places to go for ready-to-wear and many smaller chains and independent haberdashers as well as the bespoke or custom shops." The list of options in New York gets shorter when it comes to finding tweeds. There are second-hand stores certainly, but honestly, how easy would it be to find something in Will's lean and statuesque dimensions?

"To this day, one of my shopping regrets is not buying this beautiful Savile Row bespoke gun club check tweed suit, which I found at a vintage shop. It fit me perfectly, but it had the highest rise trousers I have ever tried on," he chuckles. "The waistband, in my memory, sat a clear two or three inches higher than my natural waist. At the time I thought it to be far too eccentric. But in hindsight I think I would have worn it gladly." He was able to lay his hands on a ready-to-wear green Purdey tweed jacket with a red overcheck at an East Village boutique. "It's relatively lightweight, which makes it versatile in New York. It's probably the one I've had the longest, and I've worn it a lot with wool twill trousers, corduroys and moleskins." The elusive tweed suit he wanted tailored specifically for him would be the appropriately metaphoric itch he was dying to scratch. "My parents gave me an old keeper's tweed suit with plus twos that they bought second hand for my birthday one year which I have worn on a few occasions. Unfortunately, it was just never a great fit," he sighs.

He therefore often resorted to online sellers on Ebay, which in turn, led him to other clothing enthusiasts and kindred spirits on several public internet forums. It was at one of these sites that he chanced upon the now-defunct Corduroy Appreciation Club, and out of curiosity, decided to attend one of its gatherings. For all too brief a time, the Corduroy Appreciation Club was among Gotham's ill-kept secret societies. Simultaneously serious and cheeky, the club founded by Miles Rohan in 2005 claims to have had as many as four thousand members at the peak of its glory. It came with membership cards made of, what else, corduroy, and an official logo of a whale. (See what they did there?) They had oaths, and rituals, and of course, cocktails. In the course of its existence, it exuded the kind of "insider" cachet that's catnip to New Yorkers. They were written up in the New York Times, the New Yorker, the Wall Street Journal, the Village Voice, and the Daily News. The mission statement was already there in the name, but its policy of requiring people who attend the gatherings to wear at least two items of corduroy was never rigidly enforced. Policing the members was unnecessary because underneath the feigned ceremony and irony, among them was a genuine love for the fabric with tufted cords.

One of the club speakers at the affair the night Will went was Andrew Yamato, who was then an outreach producer for New York's local PBS station WNET Thirteen. Andrew's work in providing public television multimedia content as an educational tool for teachers combined several of his personal interests in history, writing, and filmmaking. History, particularly, was the fertile ground from which he's cultivated a striking and immaculate way of dressing for which he is well regarded in New York social circles. Andrew credits the internet for finding himself running in some of those circles. As he points out, New Yorkers are inclined to seek out their particular "tribes" along whatever ground they may find shared affinity. And these days there is no faster and easier way of finding like-minded individuals than online. There was a time when the only reliable site was the message boards of Style Forum. Will concurs, though now he says, "You can do any simple internet search, that's how I found the Corduroy Appreciation Club among others. You can find so many different groups and individuals dedicated to different kinds of sartorial interests." Some of those people are New Yorkers, people like Swann Auction Galleries' George S. Lowry, vintage and antique dealer Sean Crowley, hoofer Bobby White, and yes Andrew, all known as much for their professions as for their personal styles.

Will was impressed by Andrew but was unable to meet him that evening. Instead, they ran into each other a year later at, curiously enough, the second Big Apple Tweed Ride. A kind of loose adaptation of London's annual Tweed Run, the New York version followed the original format of having participants, clad in their finest tweeds, bike around town. On a nippy Fall day, New York's tweed enthusiasts mounted their bicycles (the more vintage, the better) and snaked along at the top speed of a brisk stroll from Grand Army Plaza through Park Slope in Brooklyn. They finally convened at Flatbush Farm restaurant where an Old English-style brunch, live music, and revelry awaited. Will and Andrew, who was in good form wearing a three-piece bespoke Harris Tweed suit, instantly connected. It began with their being both partial to fine menswear. Their friendship grew on subsequent meetings and chats over history, cooking, family. Ultimately, that friendship and their interest in menswear led to working together on a mission to get Will his very own custom tweed suit.

II

Nature Patterned You and When She Was Done

The champagne of tweeds is and always will be Harris Tweed, which takes pride in its provenance as well as the manner in which it is made. As established by a trademark first granted to the Harris Tweed Association in 1909, genuine Harris Tweed has to be hand-spun, hand-woven products of 100% wool, and dyed by the crofters and cottars from the 130-mile island chain known as the Outer Hebrides: North and South Uist, Benbecula and Barra, and the Isle of Lewis and Harris. In 1993, a British Act of Parliament empowered the new Harris Tweed Authority (succeeding the association) to protect the now widely recognized orb trademark (created in 1911) and preserve the cloth's authenticity. This Harris Tweed orb trademark is dutifully stamped on every yard that is produced.

Central to the Harris Tweed industry is the Isle of Lewis and Harris. To the north, two thirds of this single landmass is the more densely-populated Lewis where the capital, Stornoway, bustles as much as a small town can on bars, hotels, and unassuming shops. An isthmus demarcates the southern one-third known as Harris, which has the more rolling topography. Exposed to mercurial assaults of ferocious gales and torrential storms from the Atlantic, the island has more than its share of wet weather. During the winter months, the plaintive and ceaseless howls of the winds are purported to induce madness. In July and August, coastal grasslands called machair are embellished by profusions of clovers, buttercups, daisies, and marsh orchids. Parts of the shoreline are fringed by beaches with undulating turquoise waters and sand dunes that can rise up to fifty feet. The shifting sands, tides, and light can so utterly and spectacularly transfigure these vistas from one moment to the next: idyllic one minute, elegiac the next.

Inland, Lewis and Harris maintains a stubborn grasp on historic remnants that predate even its Viking and Gaelic past, from ancient burial mounds and the mysterious Callanish Stones to the peat that reaches down to depths of twenty feet. A clear day lays bare the raw beauty from which Harris Tweed is decanted: exquisite rocky formations and verdant pastures bedecked by an unending diversity of flowers, picturesque crofter's cottages and the fabled blackhouses. At any moment, the volatile skies overhead may change colors from bright blue to somber gray or vibrant orange and purple. And even across the vast and profound stillness of peat bogs and desolate moors, the beating heart of the island can always be heard in the rhythmic clacks of Hattersley looms.

Seemingly in defiance of the outside world's relentless march towards a machine-coded future, Harris Tweed, or *Clò Mor* ('big cloth') in Gaelic, was initially defined by the insular nature of its very creation. Yes, certain accommodations have since been reached. The yarn still has to be 100% pure virgin wool, although it no longer needs to be hand spun nor exclusively from sheep on the islands. Originally, the wool used for Harris Tweed was from Hebridean sheep, small, often multiple-horned animals with wool ranging from soft to coarse and in colors from gray to reddish brown. The introduction of black face or Linton sheep into the region likely hastened their extinction. And today Scottish cross-breeds and Cheviot sheep have also been adopted to provide variations in the thickness and quality of fleece. More substantial fleece, for instance, could be had from the heavier sheep with longer legs accustomed to the harsher temperatures of the high moor-lands.

Shearing normally occurs from June through July when the animals' coats have grown burdensome. Shorn wool used to be colored with dyes brewed from lichen, the roots, leaves, and flowers of local plants and vegetables, and washed in the peaty waters of the islands. The yarns were woven on those cast iron looms with treadles and wooden benches ("*beart bheag*" in Gaelic) that guaranteed Harris Tweed was crafted by hand. It takes years to master the necessary skills of weaving and dyeing in the manner employed by the islanders. For instance, even when dyeing with chemicals, the method often involved use of separate pigments blended in precise amounts applied to the wool be-fore being spun into yarn. The blends may also contain several differ-ent colors to result in the desired range of tones or hues. The use of modern dyes to achieve consistency is still seen by some, however, as a disadvantage since the old way produces subtle yet altogether more pleasingly unexpected color variations.

So flinty is tweed in its initial state that it also used to be subjected to "waulking", a method some continue to perform in which the imma-ture cloth, while still wet, would be trampled upon to compact and strengthen it. Paddles then took over as convenient implements with which to bludgeon tweed into shape and submission. For generations, waulking tweed was turned into a source of merriment to ease the hard work. During the early years, the women who did the waulking gathered around a makeshift table on which they lifted and slammed down the section of cloth in front of them, pushing it around and around as they sang folk songs. Spectators also gathered about to par-ticipate in the fun by singing along or cheering the proceedings. The objective was to shrink the cloth down to an inch for every foot; and the entire process was usually accomplished in the time it took for the group to sing a certain number of songs. The cloth would then be rolled and if it could be stood on end on its own, then the work was done. Though this custom is now lost to history, it is still remembered for how tweed is entrenched in the social fabric of the island communities.

- - - - - - - - -

When the 6th Earl of Dunmore Alexander Edward Murray (1804-1845) died, his widow, Catherine, the Countess of Dunmore (1814-1886) inherited the 150,000 acres of the Dunmore estate on Harris (bought by George Murray, the 5th Earl of Dunmore (1762-1836) from Alexander Norman Macleod for £60,000 in 1834). In 1868, the Dunmore family had Amhuinnsuidhe Castle built, which still stands today. History cites the countess for vigorously championing tweed, firstly by commissioning the Murray tartan pattern woven into garments that were worn by her estate gamekeepers (although others say this was the Earl's doing); then by subsidizing the training of weavers to standardize the quality of tweed and promote its production as a local industry. She is also said to have encouraged the wearing of tweed as stylish sporting attire among her circle of aristocratic friends. But the countess was not the first to have pioneered estate tweeds, which were traditionally derived from tartans.

In the US, the words "plaid" and "tartan" are commonly and indiscriminately interchanged. Technically though, plaids can refer to something with a crisscross pattern or the material or garment itself; while tartans are the plaids with the colors and patterns of a specific clan (also referred to as a "sett"). Tartans were first observably regional since the cloth would come from the same sources. Mostly taking the form of kilts, tartans were widespread across socio-economic groups. But after the defeat of the Jacobites at the Battle of Culloden in 1746, the wearing of tartans acquired political meaning, and was suppressed to discourage the idea of another unified uprising. A year later, the British government passed the Act of Proscription under which there is a clause that has come to be known as The Dress Act, conceived to dissuade regional people from banding together through uniforms. Under threat of six-month imprisonment for first offenders and seven-year banishment to an overseas plantation for repeat offenders, it was made illegal to wear "Highland clothes". Still, by the 1800s, Highland chiefs began outfitting retainers at their estates in a distinct sett that became inextricably identified with their clan. Thus, fealty was outwardly demonstrated by wearing the clan colors. Passing those garments down to the next generation then gave families a beloved way of honoring clan continuity.

As the upkeep of Scottish estates became costly, some were either sold or rented out. In 1840 the Glenfeshie estate was tenanted by Edward Ellice M.P. (1783-1863) whose daughter-in-law was the artist Katherine Jane "Janie" Ellice (née Balfour, 1813-1864). At this time, this was not yet the imposing Glenfeshie (which recently doubled as Balmoral Castle in the 2016 Netflix series "The Crown"). Back then it was nothing more than a scattering of wooden huts, which served as lodging for the family guests. The creative Mrs. Ellice, who was acting as hostess, is said to have been distressed that she and her guests were unable to wear the tartan of the clan due to the dictates of tradition. So she decided to make her own, superimposing a red overcheck to a standard black and white Shepherd's check, and effectively designing the first estate tartan for the Glenfeshie attendants, ghillies, and gamekeepers. Nearly all the early estate tartans and tweeds were new combinations like this or variations of classic patterns.

Tweeds, in the meantime, was being produced in such varieties, its classifications began to haphazardly overlap. Those named after their place of origins include the Irish Donegal and the German Saxony (though today some Australian merino wools may also be referred to as Saxony tweeds), or Welsh or Yorkshire. Those from the kind of wool they come from are Shetland and Cheviot. Those named after their utility are called Gamekeeper or Sporting tweeds. The functional aspect of these tweeds also became another vital factor in its evolution. Since the colors and patterns were often derived from the moors, the woodland, and landscapes, an expected consequence was tweed as a means of blending into the environment.

Around 1845, a new tweed was produced, attributed to the then Lord Lovat. He was an avid sportsman who was supposed to have taken in the beauty of Loch Morar in springtime and had tweeds made to replicate the colorful mix of birch, heather, bracken, and primrose he had witnessed. The resulting blend of seven colors in varying proportions appeared like mottled camouflage. One story claims that a mill sent him a suit of this "Lovat" tweed and he reciprocated with a gift of salmon. Another lord is credited for a different pattern for concealment in the outdoors - the "Elcho mixture". It came about to correct what the then Lord Elcho thought were the too easily-spotted reds of his London Scottish Regiment soldiers' uniforms. He came up with a muted ruddy brown version, apparently resembling the soil of his native East Lothian, and is believed to have led to the creation of khaki uniforms.

No other personage could have done more to elevate tweed's stature however than Francis Albert Augustus Charles Emmanuel (1819-1861), Prince Consort to HRH Queen Victoria (1819-1901). After already having visited Scotland several times with the Queen, Prince Albert purchased the Balmoral estate in 1848 from the Inverey Farquharsons. Here the royal couple had Balmoral Castle built as their country home. During her first visit, the Queen noted in her journals that it was "small but pretty". Years of extensive construction was undertaken for a larger house that could shelter staff, official visitors, and friends. Since the royal couple was only too aware that people would take offense to English nobles donning any existing clan tartan, Prince Albert decided to commission one specifically for deer stalking, and as his way of honoring Highland traditions. Prior to the Queen laying down the castle's foundation stone in 1853, a Balmoral tartan was already designed and woven into tweed: a nearly black shade of blue with white and crimson. It is alleged to simulate the rugged texture of Cairngorms' granite mountains.

As word of the goings-on at Balmoral spread from ear to eager ear among Londoners, a new era in tweed began. Soon, those who were listed on Burke's Peerage would think it obligatory to scurry high and wide in search of a country homestead they could call their own. Not long after, anyone with even the most tenuous claims to a title, or simply possessed by the most dogged of social aspirations would convince themselves they too had to have a place in the country. And if there wasn't anything quite appropriate to be found, newly wealthy industrialists had one built to spec. Many estate houses and hunting lodges rose on once virgin tracts of land like mushrooms after rainfall. Of course, to give it the requisite legitimacy, an estate had to have its own tweed, giving rise to ever more patterns and color combinations. Because after all, even those who couldn't tell grouse from pheasant still needed to be dressed in tweeds.

By the late 1800s, Scottish tweed (and tartans) was being copied and marketed in less expensive versions by everyone from the English to the French. This led to tweeds all but losing their use as exclusive signifiers of a family or estate. The tartans and patterns, as woven in more accessible fabrics, were easily replicated by machinery such as the new Jacquard loom. Somehow though, even as it gained mass popularity, tweed's association with the aristocracy and the leisure class also gathered further momentum. In 1840, Caroline Stuart, Countess of Seafield (1830-1911) outfitted her retainers at the Seafield estate in the tweeds with the Glenurquhart check. Queen Victoria's son Albert Edward (1841-1910), the Prince of Wales, (also known informally as "Bertie"), who was a regular guest of the Seafields, took interest. He is said to have been so taken by the pattern that he had garments made but added red-brown and white with navy to delineate the different sections of the check. This came to be known as the Prince of Wales Check.

Bertie was no intellectual. But he was widely admired for having a certain facility for international diplomacy. Much to the consternation of his parents however, during Bertie's protracted wait to be crowned Edward VII, he also gained a well-earned reputation as a near mythic playboy and style icon. Many of his fashion choices are as well chronicled as his dalliances with society hostess Alice Keppel (1868-1947), the actress Lillie Langtry (1853-1929), and countless other women. His overall popularity was such that even the French shamelessly copied his manner of dressing.

One of his many contributions to style still in practice today was leaving the bottom button of his waistcoat unfastened, which he did to accommodate a mid section that was getting more pronounced. He is also credited for the smoking jacket, and shifting popular taste away from white tails to evening jackets after wearing a dark blue one with black trousers and bow tie at dinner. Whenever he stayed at the spa destination Marienbad, tailors reportedly showed up to spy for any changes in his style that they assumed might become the next trend. When he was spotted wearing a green Tyrolean hat, it became a best-seller. The Norfolk jacket and the Homburg hat both became in demand as a result of being worn by Bertie. After Bertie ascended the throne, Sir Winston Churchill (1874-1965) once proclaimed matter-of-factly that everyone wore tweeds to the Goodwood Races, "following the king's sensible example."

When the Prince of Wales pattern became available on Savile Row, the middle classes of the Edwardian era wholeheartedly embraced it as a desirable look for the proper English city gentleman, even as tweeds continued to be *'de rigueur'* among the sporting, country estate set. The estates themselves however proved much more difficult to sustain. After the devastating world wars, most of these baronial buildings were converted into barracks, hospitals, schools, or housing for evacuees. Taxes, the costs of structural upkeep, maintaining live-in service, lack of proper plumbing or wiring for electricity, and the expense of heating expansive and drafty rooms all contributed to ravaging many of these homes. As the number of estates dwindled, so too did the need to outfit staff in tweeds. But the torch the leisure set had always carried for tweeds was picked up, then set ablaze by a most unexpected proponent from the continent. And it was a Frenchwoman, no less.

- - - - - - - -

Despite being more closely aligned with presumed male-oriented outdoorsy activities, tweeds have always been worn by women too, of course. This fact would simply attain a higher profile as women swaddled in tweeds began participating in cycling and golf. But it was in the hands of a brilliant couturier that tweed achieved its most iconic look in women's wear. Gabrielle "Coco" Chanel (1883-1971) first earned recognition for emancipating women from the constricting corsets that had characterized women's wear during La Belle Époque. Other leading couturiers of the era such as Elsa Schiaparelli (1890-1973) and Cristóbal Balenciaga (1895-1972) either mesmerized with surrealistic creations or was celebrated for upholding the grandest traditions of couture with phenomenal tailoring skills. Chanel, on the other hand, offered relaxed, pragmatic clothes, sophisticated in their simplicity yet indubitably luxurious. Chanel was also singular in openly subverting accepted gender norms by appropriating what were then taken for granted as aspects of menswear and using them for women's wear. For instance, the jersey knits she commissioned from Jacques Rodier (the grandson of Eugene Rodier, who founded the brand bearing the family name as a manufacturing company in 1848) for her collections were originally intended for making men's underwear. Chanel's concept, as manifested by her women's riding breeches and blazers, was nothing less than revolutionary and shockingly modern at the time.

Chanel is said to have developed her initial fascination for British menswear during her relationship with the businessman and polo player Captain Arthur "Boy" Capel (1881-1919) who backed the venture to start her fashion line. Years after his passing, Chanel met yet another Englishman who extended her enterprise even further. It was Christmas in Monaco when Chanel first met Hugh Grosvenor (1879-1953) the 2nd Duke of Westminster, who everyone called Bendor. Almost from their first dinner aboard his boat "Flying Cloud," which conveniently laid at anchor in Monaco, through most of their relationship, the speculation of a possible marriage hovered over them. And though they never did wed, their lives would thereafter be linked in many ways.

Bendor was among the richest men in Britain, of a restless disposition, and accustomed to getting his way. Many mutual friends (including Winston Churchill) claimed that they made a good couple since Chanel very easily matched Bendor's daring temperament. At Bendor's Lochmore Lodge property in the Highlands, records show Chanel as having been a frequent guest and participant in salmon fishing expeditions. There, Chanel was photographed with her catch, casually and comfortably attired in Bendor's tweeds. It's not much of a reach to suppose it was probably then that Chanel gave thought to using the cloth alongside the knit jerseys for her designs. And she eventually found the perfect source in Linton Tweeds.

In the early part of the 1900s, William Linton, originally from Hawick, was already well trained in the production of tweeds by the time he set up Linton Tweeds in Carlisle. From a small two-story building, the mill gradually grew to include several nearby red brick structures housing some 100 employees. In those days, Linton Tweeds was represented by salesmen who trekked around in pony traps to nearby outfitters. But it wasn't long before the mill's well crafted materials won over many of even the far-off and haughtiest of couture houses. Its clients came to count the likes of Schiaparelli, Edward Molyneaux (1891-1974), and Jean Patou (1880-1936). It is said that Molyneaux was the one who introduced Linton to Chanel, thus starting a generations-long relationship between the mill and the house.

In 1925, Chanel unveiled her now signature tweed ensemble, which takes on average 150 hours to make. The rich, textured material is cut in simple, fluid lines to hang on instead of wrapping itself around the body, forever removing any literal context to the expression of looking "pulled together". Two years later, Chanel set up shop in London to much fanfare among the upper classes. Her relationship with Bendor had already opened doors for her there and British high society was more than receptive to what mademoiselle had to offer. Her standing was further cemented after British Vogue ran a photograph of the baroness Édouard de Rothschild, Germaine Halphen (1884-1975) in a Chanel suit captioned "Tweeds have made the practical beautiful and the beautiful practical".

Chanel's fidelity to creating uncomplicated garments, her fierce ambition, and the clarity with which she understood her market all contributed to her unstoppable ascent. It was also particularly astute to distance herself from the more widely expected role of a subservient dressmaker, becoming instead a style arbiter, whose every imperious edict was followed to the capital "C". Before Bendor married for a third time, (rumored to have been precipitated by the need to secure an heir) Chanel begrudgingly received her lover's future wife Loelia Ponsonby at her apartment. Ponsonby, who was among the clique of hard-partying British aristos dubbed by the press as "Bright Young Things", later wrote in her memoir of feeling intimidated by being presented to the designer. She felt as though she was being inspected and if she could pass muster. The soon-to-be Duchess of Westminster summed it up with, "I doubt very much whether I, or my tweed suit, was suitable."

- - - - - - - - -

By the 1920s, tweed had achieved wider popularity after being worn by athletes and other prominent public figures. Mountaineer George Herbert Leigh Mallory (1886-1924), for one, tried (although failed) to conquer Mt. Everest wearing a three-piece Harris Tweed suit. Thomas Mitchell Morris (1821-1908), the Scottish golfer called Old Tom Morris, wore only tweed plus fours when he played and it became thereafter the golf wear of choice by both men and women well into the 1930s. But tweed made its first significant crossing to the New World in the 1920s along with several other items in the British menswear canon when American students brought them back Stateside after studying at Oxford or Cambridge. One such item, for example, was the Cambridge rowing team's blazers, so named because of the original jacket's red color. The Americans understandably assimilated what the local students wore at these institutions of learning. And they likely continued to wear the same clothes once they were back home to exude an air of acquired European sophistication. Between the two world wars, tweed suits, blazers, Shetland pullovers and others articles of clothing were gradually codified into the totality of what came to be known as the Ivy League look.

The term "Ivy League" was coined for the athletic conference participated in by private universities in the East Coast. It came to be wider known in reference to most everything about these schools from a dedication to academic excellence to elitism. The word "look" seems to have first been appended on record long after this manner of dressing had already worked its way past the confines of the prestigious quads, pep rallies, and eating clubs. In fact it had already spread to other American schools and even to the older generation when the phrase first appeared in print. The expression showed up in the November 22, 1954 issue of Life Magazine with a cover touting the splendor of color television. Inside was the feature (sans a byline) declaring "The Ivy Look Heads Across U.S." and "Natural-shouldered suit becomes a new male uniform". This being Life magazine, the story was accompanied by some wonderful photographs including one of New York publicist Patrick O'Higgins wearing a suit captioned as "moderate Edwardian British riding clothes (combined) with a guardsman's uniform", which featured slanted pockets and cuffed trousers. Another showed a handsome Yaley called James M. Brown III being fitted with a tweed jacket by an anonymous tailor. Interestingly, the same issue has a second fashion story spotlighting the then 28-year old designer James Galanos showing off one of his tweed coat dress designs.

Another such style migration were the regulation American military khakis (traceable back to Lord Elcho), which were eventually enfolded into the unofficial collegiate uniform. Other items that grew in popularity by the 1950s and 1960s were button-down Oxford shirts and crew neck sweaters. But it's likewise important to note that the Ivy League look had less to do with the items themselves. Simply having on a cable knit sweater, for example, wasn't enough. The look was infinitely greater than the sum of its parts and always dictated by how the students put everything together into peer-approved ensembles worn under the right conditions.

The Ivy League look is anchored by a little bit of anglophilia, a dash of sports, and a liberal amount of the social activities at the big three universities – Princeton (Est. 1746), Harvard(Est. 1636), and Yale (Est. 1701). But as in all fashion movements of any significance, it's not a style so easily reduced to an overnight sensation of a trend, nor simplified for having served a sole function. A complex mix of fashion items, societal circumstances, the youth culture of the era, and canny merchandisers all pushed and pulled at each other for years to unwittingly conspire in its creation. The looks imported from the UK were reoriented in more casually American yet no less privileged ways and placed in youth oriented settings. Retailers like Brooks Brothers and Gant responded with as many Americanized British staples as they could churn out. But not everything passed the discriminating tastes of their target market. Certain items were ignored while others became synonymous to the Ivy League look such as cardigans, blazers, chinos, Weejun loafers, and yes, tweeds. At some point, the retailers began taking their leads on what to manufacture based mostly (if not entirely) on what the kids were wearing. They constantly monitored the campus wardrobes of the big three, with Princeton students as the acknowledged and most trusted of style setters.

Among the many retailers that attempted to embody the Ivy League look, none were as true to the aesthetic as J.Press. The likeliest of explanations is that it didn't have to feel the pulse of its market, sitting as it did on a carotid artery of one of the elite institutions. Founded by Jacobi Press in 1902, the flagship store opened at Harvard on Auburn Street in the 1930s. Since then it has consistently offered Repp ties, dartless sack jackets, and herringbone tweed Chesterfield overcoats (named after the 6th Earl of Chesterfield George Stanhope, 1805-1866). Not to be outdone, Brooks Brothers had its salesmen crisscrossing the Northeast corridor to ply their merchandise to prep school and college students, while smaller outfitters like the Andover Shop in Cambridge would be content providing for the men within its close environs. In its over a century history, J. Press has opened, closed, and re-opened stores in New York City and unfortunately had to shutter its Cambridge location in 2018. Today, having been acquired by fashion industry stalwart Onward Kashiyama, it still has brick and mortar stores in New Haven, Washington DC, and midtown New York, and thrives online with a healthy market in Japan.

The traditional Ivy League jacket was of heavy (usually worsted) wool, single breasted with narrow notched lapels and patch pockets. It was soon joined by herringbone tweeds and striped Cheviot versions. Warm though they were, wool flannel trousers and navy blue flannel jackets were once commonly donned in the summer for yachting. Another key aspect in which tweed played an important role was the students' preference for countrified looks especially when school opened in the Fall. At the basest level, a garment aimed at Ivy Leaguers had to be appropriate for participating in or watching their favored sporting pursuits like crew, polo, lacrosse, fencing, riding, tennis. But, and this is the part most retailers fail to comprehend, the point was never about looking rich or even particularly refined. It's about ultimately looking insouciant, as though one just threw something on with the barest of an inconvenient afterthought. It's the madras shirt for summering in the Cape, or the sweater flung carelessly over the shoulders to cram for finals, or the loafers once worn with argyle socks but now never ever with any socks at all.

- - - - - - - -

Tweed has always been well disposed in evincing a demeanor of old money, aided in part by every *ancien régime*'s aversion to anything shiny and new. All the more ironic that French designer Christian Dior (1905-1957) would launch his career with a couture collection dubbed the "New Look" by the hyperventilating fashion press when it would've been more accurate to call it the "Old Look". In February 1947, Dior's "Corolla Line" of unabashedly feminine dresses, cinched at the waist, with overflowing skirts debuted to unstinting raves. A reporter from Reuters is said to have tossed her story down from a window of the Avenue Montaigne couture house to a waiting messenger on the street below in order for it to make the US presses on the same day. Dior has publicly admitted that his inspiration was drawn mostly from the dresses his mother had worn to the races at Deauville in the 1900s. But coming out after the frugality and stringent rationing of the second world war, this return to elegance was a welcome breath of extravagant air. Alongside the meters of tulle and chiffon were voluminous woolen suiting fabric, which Dior would shape into ultra feminine, geometric marvels he tagged by the silhouette: the Y Line, the Arrow Line and so on.

But his most lasting tweed appears on the bottle of his Miss Dior fragrance. Created by perfumers Paul Vacher, Serge Heftler Louiche, and Jean Carles, the fragrance was worldly, thus surprisingly counter-intuitive to the innocent, floral theme of the season's collection when it was unveiled. Composed of 350 ingredients, the scent has a green aldehydic top, followed by a narcotic floral heart, and finishing with a warm, mossy base to evoke Parisian (town) sophistication and Provençal (country) sensuality. Its original amphora bottle was de-signed by Fernand Guéry-Colas (1902-1957) and produced by Baccarat in clear crystal, overlaid in enamels, then housed in silk-lined boxes. But overwhelming demand urged Parfums Dior to rethink the costly packaging. Architect Victor Grandpierre, who had designed chez Dior, recommended using one of the tweeds from the collection as the motif for the redesign. A new rectangular bottle was cut with a houndstooth pattern embossed on frosted crystal, its facets allowing the liquid within to flicker in the light. The houndstooth design in black and white is repeated on the cap and the box as an added elegant touch.

Decades later, the House of Creed would forego allusion altogether with the introduction of its fragrance "Green Irish Tweed". Creed was originally founded in 1760 London by custom tailor James Henry Creed to make garments for the royal court of Great Britain. Scents were first added to the merchandise because George William Frederick (1738-1820), otherwise known as King George III, had taken a shine to the scented leather gloves they had made for him. So much so he com-missioned a personalized fragrance based on the scent. That first formula, called "Royal English Leather", was composed of mandarin, ambergris, and sandalwood. Twenty years later, Queen Victoria appointed Creed an official supplier to the court and it has since made numerous personal fragrances for the crowned heads of Europe including Eugénie de Montijo (1826-1920) the last Empress of France, and Franz-Josef I (1830–1916), Emperor of Austria, Apostolic King of Hungary, and King of Bohemia. Nearly two centuries later, Creed finally made its exclusive fragrances available to the public when it opened a flagship store in Paris. To this day, it's still a family company, privately held by sixth generation Olivier Creed, and son Erwin, who someday will undoubtedly advance his family's legacy.

Green Irish Tweed went onto the shelves in 1985, appropriately and concomitantly conveying Creed's pedigree in both luxury and tailoring. Whether or not the immediate success of the fragrance had anything to do with how well it captures tweed in an olfactory way may be a subjective matter. Aficionados find the pronounced aquatic quality of the top notes a bit removed from the cloth. Still, everyone agrees the sheer sophistication of its accord of violet leaves, Florentine iris, ambergris, and sandalwood provides excellent projection and sillage.

- - - - - - -

Curiously, no one at Parfums Chanel has ever ventured to concoct a scent to conceptually capture its tweed suit. It isn't quite clear why Chanel held but a paltry ten percent stake in the business with majority shares owned by the *freres* Wertheimer, Pierre and Paul. Nevertheless, by the 1950s when she was already in retirement, profits from the fragrance line were enough to keep Chanel in tweeds and pearls for a few lifetimes. Still, at 71 years old, she seemed to have found herself bored by inactivity that she suddenly decided to reopen her salon with the idea of spotlighting the seminal tweed suit to mark her return to fashion.

At this point, Chanel had already perfected her *métier*, having spent decades refining her signature styles. The three-piece look of blouse, jacket, and skirt was among her bestsellers and she counted on it being her comeback look. The blouse was color coordinated with the lining of the cardigan-like jacket. The jacket was tailored with high armholes to facilitate arm movements, equipped with pockets, hung just to the hip, and weighed down by a gilt chain stitched along the inside hem. The matching skirt fell to the knee and was lined on the back panel to preserve the seat of the garment. Jacket and skirt were usually trimmed with braid. Completing the look were lavish details: jeweled cuff links, double C logo buttons (or in brass lion heads), chain belts, and necklaces of cabochon clusters. Also closely recognized as part of the look were the multiple strands of pearls with which Chanel festooned herself (gifts from Bendor that arrived one rope for every birthday).

But when she showed her latest collection in 1954, the French fashion editors were unimpressed. To describe the reviews as having been unpleasant would be equating a fender bender to the Titanic hitting an iceberg. They were mercilessly savage. The assumption is everyone came for some sort of grand revelation of fashion's future. Those heightened expectations were inescapable, yet inevitably impossible to have been met with satisfaction. To be fair, nothing short of an epiphany is what all fashion faithful look for in any show. What they found at Chanel that day instead, however fine tuned, was to them an unexceptional retreading of already well traversed ground.

Across the pond, it was an altogether different story. True, the Chanel suit was already familiar in rarefied circles since the 1930s. But prior to the 1950s Chanel wasn't exactly a household name. Suddenly, however, the middle class was there and being told that they too could have things that used to be the *accoutrements* of only the very rich. Or at least, buy passable facsimiles. And to these Americans, flush with newfound prosperity and striving to upmarket themselves, Chanel was the ne plus ultra of chic. The clothes were so unaffected and easy. Eager to satiate the public demand, garment businesses on Seventh Avenue recreated the suit, albeit often in less expensive fabrics. There was a system in place then when manufacturers bought the "rights" from the Paris fashion houses to reproduce their designs in the US under a different label. And if it were feasible, the manufacturer would order the same material from the mills. Regardless of the knock offs, there was enough business on the Chanel suit to reinvigorate the brand itself, and by extension, ensured that Linton Tweeds and other tweed mills would receive hefty orders of its cloth from the US.

But as the children of the 1950s came of age by the late 1960s through the 1970s, they would predictably repudiate the values of the previous generation. And both the Chanel and Ivy League looks fell victim to this phenomenon. They were inescapably deemed anachronistic following a series of social, political and cultural upheavals from the assassination of President John F. Kennedy (1917-1963) and Watergate to the Vietnam War and the rise of mod and hippie cultures, sexual liberation, as well as the civil, women's, and gay rights movements. The naïve sanguinity of previous decades was purged with violence and uncertainty in hopes of ushering in a new world. Along the way, fuel to the raging rejection of presumed "norms" were boundary pushing literature, abstract expressionism and pop art, new wave cinema, punk and disco music. Collectively, these rendered nearly everything that had come before almost irretrievably obsolete. Almost. Tweeds, along with corduroys, and even velvets, were deprived of their previous connotations through reconfigured cuts and silhouettes and appropriated as subversive looks. The avant-garde, intellectuals, and bohemians were all attired in tweeds to look purposely disheveled and unrepentantly louche.

In 1969, a musical called "Coco" starring film star Katharine Hepburn (1907-2003) as Chanel was mounted on Broadway at the former Mark Hellinger Theatre. With book and lyrics by Alan Jay Lerner (1918-1986) and music by André Previn (1929-2019), it was based on Chanel's life, however loosely, considering the number of apocryphal stories she herself proliferated. Sir Cecil Beaton (1904-1980) was engaged to create the sets and costumes. Throughout the production, Hepburn and Sir Cecil had such a contentious relationship that the actress is said to have bought clothes from Chanel behind his back in case the costumes he designed were not to her liking. One, a white tweed suit, reportedly appeared during the run of the show. But times had changed and the show dropped its final curtain after only a little over 300 performances. Sir Cecil, meanwhile, won an Antoinette Perry Award (better known as a Tony) for the costumes.

Two years later, before she completed her Spring 1971 collection, Chanel passed away. The brand lived on. The succeeding generations of Wertheimers (first Jacques, then Alain) took over and eventually appointed Karl Lagerfeld (1993-2019) as creative director. He mined some of the house's cherished looks and rather skillfully endowed them with the brashness of the new era. In January 1983, he debuted with a couture collection detached from the very proper ladies of the past but was somehow still so very Chanel. As the surety of Lagerfeld's handling of the brand increased so too did his irreverent use of flamboyant accessories, short skirts, and Linton tweeds in strikingly modern powdery pastels and jewel tones. But they all worked because he had sense enough not to yield to parody, presenting these instead as a valid progression of the Chanel style.

- - - - - - - -

Linton Tweeds, meanwhile, had done well even after William Linton died in 1938. His sole offspring Agnes, who had been by her father's side through it all, took over the business. She was followed by a Linton cousin, George, who had regularly traveled with Agnes to Paris and the US to meet with clients and show them the latest designs. In 1969, to oversee mill operations, George hired Leslie Walker (1934-2014) whose grandfather had opened Heather Mills in Selkirk in 1892. Leslie implemented much needed changes to improve the mill's operations. But by the time Australian model Patricia Dow wore a tweed Anne Klein blazer for the cover of the July 1, 1971 edition of American Vogue, sales of tweeds to the US had near completely unraveled.

The following year, the Linton family voted to hold on to minor shareholder stakes in the company while relinquishing controlling shares to Leslie Walker. He had to borrow the money to complete the purchase and it was not a propitious beginning. Compounding the matter of changing tastes in the 1970s, Leslie's son and current managing director Keith Walker explains, "There were also labor related issues going on in New York then, and my father frantically scrambled to find other markets." But find it he did - in Japan. A gentleman called Taka Uchinuma proved invaluable in cultivating a strong presence for Linton Tweeds there. Because of the steady demand for Linton Tweeds in that country, a partnership was set up with Uchinuma-san that became Linton Japan. Even the loss-leading couture houses helped the bottom line when they began opening ready-to-wear categories that produced tweed garments in less pricey versions.

During his father's early tenure at Linton Tweeds, Keith spent summers working at its showroom. In most family businesses, children following after their parents' footsteps is a foregone conclusion. Not so in this case. "I was always eager to work here," Keith says. "But my father had very serious reservations because he felt it was too risky a business." Instead, the older Walker nudged Keith towards banking. Still, Keith persisted and earned his place in the company, becoming its commercial director in 1988. He was appointed managing director in 1994 when Leslie stepped down. And the legacy will surely continue since Keith's sons Duncan and Ross are already working for the company.

Today, all around the 60,000 square-foot expanse of the Linton Tweeds facilities, there are tear sheets and framed fashion spreads, ad campaigns, and paparazzi shots of the boldface names who've been photographed in cloth manufactured in these premises: the late Diana, Princess of Wales (1961-1997), Caroline, Princess of Hanover, film star Nicole Kidman, and the supermodels Cindy Crawford, Naomi Campbell, Kate Moss, and Stella Tenant. There are some eighty people in production ceaselessly working the Dornier rapier looms, with four designers led by Irene Steele (who succeeded house designer Robert Irvine), and handweavers whose job is to develop original Linton Tweed patterns as well as the fabrics created exclusively for fashion houses. "We usually come out with three hundred designs per season. We can start by showing our original patterns and more often than not the designers will love them," Keith says. "But to more closely apply to their collections, they will ask us to make minor adjustments like adding an extra stripe here or change one color there." Others however will ask that new patterns be made based on a vague concept or color scheme. Here, there are a couple of wooden hand looms on which a sample can somewhat quickly be made for review by clients before being produced in larger volumes.

The patronage of the couture houses is of tremendous value to Linton Tweeds. There is no underestimating the prestige of supplying the material for the likes of Chanel, Balenciaga, Lanvin, Burberry, and even the department store Bergdorf Goodman. But Keith has hedged his bets with customers in many other countries like Russia and Germany. He adds, "We're also seeing growth in Korea and China where the interest in luxury goods hasn't slowed down." Another growing sector is the brand's end consumer channel Linton Direct. Launched in 2010, Linton Direct is able to utilize surplus materials while allowing anyone to shop online for the brand's coveted fabrics in smaller quantities. Keith says, "We get orders from everywhere, Canada, Singapore, from everyday folks or small businesses. And we encourage our customers to send us pictures of what they do with the fabric whether they made their own garments, blankets, or even jackets for their pets." Linton Direct has also introduced the brand's own scarves, small purses, and even throw pillows.

Because they specialize in loose weave tweeds commonly called in the trade as "novelty and fantasy fabrics", up to 99% of their output are made specifically for women's wear with the rest allocated toward major menswear brands like Thom Browne, high end interior design projects, as well as a range of products from shoes to handbags. Though most of the wool they use come from Yorkshire, some two-thirds of their output use yarns sourced from Italy, Germany, Japan and France. In order to keep producing new designs on schedule, the wool is subjected to Linton Tweeds' onsite twisting machines to come up with its own yarns. And it's in how the yarns are blended together, or even dyed that results in the unique variety of Linton Tweed patterns. Its five pressure package dyeing machines give the brand the capabilities of either dyeing the yarn before weaving, or weaving the material first and then piece dyed. Although they produce tweeds from light to heavier weights, the average weight of Linton Tweeds' fabric is 300 grams per square meter (or approximately nine ounces per square yard).

The necessity of constantly creating new patterns keeps Keith open to new ideas. In 2016, he incorporated the use of the German textile machinery manufacturer Groz-Beckert's PosiLeno system to increase the speed and assortment that can be produced by Linton Tweeds. Lifting frames attached to the loom enables the weaver to interlace a loose yet stable leno weave with a traditional heavier dobby weave. Keith enthuses, "It gives us the ease of knitwear manufacturing and helps us create more open-weaves for lighter weight fabrics. We can even give materials the appearance of movement." But he is also quick to say he only regards these as a supplement to and a means of improving traditional methods. He insists, "We'll never sacrifice our reputation for quality in this exclusive end of the market."

- - - - - - - - -

Lagerfeld and Linton weren't unaccompanied in taking tweed to the modern arena of designer ready-to-wear. But no one could have done more to render the cloth in radically new ways while respecting and retaining its cultural import than Vivienne Westwood, DBE RDI. The year Chanel died, Westwood and Malcolm McLaren (1946-2010) opened their boutique "Let it Rock" at 430 Kings Road with punk as its founding ethos. But they were canny enough, or young and naive enough, perhaps even arrogant enough, or even all of those enough to keep mutating the merchandise according to their interests - from rocker to biker duds to sexually graphic T shirts. And the shop's name changed accordingly ("Too Fast to Live Too Young to Die" then "Sex and Seditionaries") before finally settling as Dame Westwood's solely-owned "World's End".

After the couple parted and McLaren moved on to his musical endeavors, Westwood astonished everyone by launching collection after collection of pure ingenuity. Her pieces were remarkable for their staunch "British-ness" despite having been adroitly deconstructed and stripped of upper class sanctimony. True, Westwood's punk sensibilities suggested she was caricaturing formalized British dressing, but devoid of strident purpose, the collections were viewed as brilliant redefinitions. Even the confrontational sexuality of the angular silhouettes, the exaggerated bustles, busts, and platform heels seem posed more as question marks than exclamation points. For all their flagrant provocations and having one foot firmly planted past the line of orthodoxy, they were always delivered with a cheeky wink.

Besides, had Westwood not been adamant about her respect for the fabrics and their cultural trappings, her work certainly served as a glowing testament to them. Following her celebrated Spring Summer 1985 introduction of the mini-crini, a shortened crinoline with plastic boning, she created an Autumn version in crimson Harris Tweed, styled with a matching jacket. A couple of years later she went no-holds-barred with a collection aptly called "Harris Tweed" (the one where corsets were used as outerwear) highlighting woolen suits, capes, skirts, and riding jackets, and a royal crown made entirely of tweed. (Any controversy over the crown was relegated behind-the-scenes because while everyone knows famed milliner Stephen Jones, OBE collaborated with the designer on the crown, Westwood is allegedly sensitive to its attribution.) Through the years, the virtues of tweeds, tartans, Scottish traditions and British tailoring have been repeatedly extolled by Westwood's increasingly brilliant designs from mini kilts and a re-imagination of the Norfolk Suit to her Autumn 1993's "Anglomania" collection. In the process, the designer demonstrated how tweed need not be merely about rhapsodizing what was, and that with intrepid handling, it could still reach heretofore unforeseen heights toward a beckoning world of incalculable possibilities.

III

Crazy 'bout a Sharp Dressed
Man

A suit succeeds or fails on how the shoulders are constructed. Here is where intent is decided, stipulating how the rest of the suit's parts arrive at an agreement and take conclusive shape. The most recognized shoulder expressions are referred to as being American, British, or Italian (with degrees of differentiations and overlaps for sporty or formal looks, and everything in between). A casual appearance requires less structured shoulders, and conversely, one that needs to emit authority demands more. The contours should be directed by the wearer's body. Someone with sloping shoulders might benefit with some padding. Someone with a lanky built may wish to have a slightly extended shoulder line.

A properly made suit is one of graceful eloquence, its crafting a carefully orchestrated symphony of designated movements. One wrong note is all it takes for a seam to break or a button to disengage. The stitching has to be just so to maintain the right tension holding everything together. Too tight and irregularities will appear along the seams. Equilibrium must be achieved between the stability of the outer part of the garment and the body's ability to move within its internal structure. The pressure exerted during steam pressing differs according to its parts. The amount applied on the front of a jacket is not the same as what it would be for the trousers. Overdo the pressing and a dented outline might appear underneath the lapels, or the entire suit may come out flat, or worse still, lend the fabric a cheapening shine. These are just some of the countless particulars of which the average shopper is unaware. But from the modest ready-to-wear to the loftiest of bespoke, the finished product will bear tell-tale signs of having been made by either a good or not quite satisfactory haberdasher.

In the US, a haberdasher is a men's outfitter; while in the UK, the word refers to vendors of sewing items (known there as "haberdashery", what is called "notions" in the US). Among the most well known American haberdashers, Brooks Brothers lays claim to being the oldest, founded in 1818 by Henry Sands Brooks (1772-1883) with a store that opened on the corner of Catherine and Cherry streets in Lower Manhattan. After his death, the business was inherited by his sons who carried on under the name Brooks Brothers and trademarked the still-in-use logo of a sheep suspended by a ribbon. The symbol, with its links to long ago wool merchants in Britain, was meant to signal the shop's goals. After being in the family for over a century, the business changed hands a few times and is now privately owned by Italian billionaire Claudio del Vecchio, who is reportedly trying to revitalize the brand's image.

- - - - - - - - -

The prospect of having a tweed suit especially made for Will entered the realm of attainability the moment his good friend Andrew, who had been freelancing as a writer and filmmaker, landed a new job at Alan Flusser. "After leaving PBS, the flexible hours of freelancing gave me leeway to act as the primary caregiver to my daughter Vivian (while wife Jenny Gage worked as a private investigator) and it was a great way to balance my commitments," he recounts. But when the opening at Alan Flusser came up, it was the right job at the right time for Andrew. This exciting new position naturally brought the topic of Will's dream suit to the forefront of their ceaseless conversations about clothes. "There's no other person I trust more than Andrew when it comes to the right clothes," Will says. "When he started working at Alan's, it just occurred to me how he might be able to help me figure out the best way to get a custom tweed suit."

Of New York City's purveyors of menswear, there are haberdashers, and then there's Alan Flusser. Renowned among the gentlemanly circles of fashion, Alan earned his Prince of Wales checks in the 1970s, styling for Phillips-Van Heusen (while attending night classes at the Fashion Institute of Technology and Parsons School of Design) and then serving as head designer for the American sportswear division of Pierre Cardin. He ascribes much of his devotion to his craft to growing up around his father's exacting clothes sense. A real estate executive by profession, "He was a dandy," Alan candidly states. "And he always believed that in order to succeed, you had to look successful." Alan launched his eponymous brand in 1978 and achieved several milestones throughout the 1980s. His seminal guide in demystifying menswear - "Making the Man: The Insider's Guide to Buying Men's Clothes" - was published in 1981, for which he earned a special Cutty Sark Fashion Award. He also won a 1985 Coty Award as America's Best Menswear Designer. A year later, he opened the first Alan Flusser Custom Shop, which has taken different forms through the years up to its current one headquartered at a studio in midtown.

Shortly after setting up shop, he received a call from award-winning costume designer Ellen Mirojnick, who was working on the Oliver Stone motion picture "Wall Street". Though she already had a strong vestiary vision for the project, she must have known it would benefit the picture to have Alan add legitimacy to the main character's looks. So she entreated Alan to work on the film's headliner Michael Douglas. After Alan met with Douglas, he quickly realized this was going to be more than just putting an actor in the right suits. In order for Douglas to adequately assume his role, Alan spent three weeks judiciously drawing the actor into his milieu. Alan had him try on a slew of shirts, suits, ties, pocket squares, and cufflinks, not just to see what looked best but to gauge how Douglas responded to them.

According to Alan, the 1930s was the original point of reference he used for crafting and collating a wardrobe integral to the actor's portrayal of an alpha corporate predator. Colored shirts with white contrast cuffs and collars would command everyone's undivided attention. Pleated trousers paired with shoulder-padded jackets centered Douglas' Gordon Gekko character in a "powerfully proportioned" frame. But it was undoubtedly one of Alan's practical calibrations that provided the most memorable *pièce de résistance*. The braces intended to compensate for Douglas' slim hips ably held up his trousers while adding the kind of swaggering flourish that indelibly stamped the ensembles as the "power look" of the decade.

In addition to Douglas' costumes, another suit was made by Alan for actor Terence Stamp who played Sir Larry Wildman, a more calculatingly restrained but no less rapacious businessman. The success of the film instigated brazen imitations of the costumes. The ones Alan created for Douglas - the suits, braces, shirts, and ties - were all reproduced *ad nauseum* by other brands throughout the 1980s. But few could sufficiently copy the aggressive yet tasteful items Alan cheekily describes as "fuck you clothes". Others wisely offered fashions segregated by polar sides of the era's menswear spectrum: the *perbene* stylings of Giorgio Armani or the baroque extravagance of Gianni Versace. Of course, all good things must come to an end, including greed, as it were.

By stroke of synchronistic timing, the cultural changeover that ended the era was heralded by the publishing of a book at the close of 1989. Bryan Burrough and John Helyar's bestseller "Barbarians at the Gate: The Fall of RJR Nabisco" was reportage at its most incisive, detailing how "mercenaries, warriors clad in $2,000 Alan Flusser suits" battled over tobacco and food conglomerate RJR Nabisco. As the company lay open to a hostile takeover, it became the locus of byzantine machinations and egos run amok. The incident was revisited four years later in an HBO film by Glenn Jordan from a script by Larry Gelbart (1928-2009), with suits for actors Jonathan Pryce (who played Henry Kravis), Fred Dalton Thompson (1942-2015) (as James D. Robinson III, then chairman of American Express), and Peter Riegert (as Peter A. Cohen, then chairman of Shearson Lehman Brothers) all provided by none other than Alan Flusser. The HBO version was equally well received though not for the guilty pleasures to be had from competing network television shows like "Dynasty" or "Dallas". Instead, it was a damning indictment of the excess driven era and its Reaganomics-bred parvenus. Moot point though since by then the public had already moved on to grunge anyway.

Titans of industry still come knocking at Alan's door, of course. That never stopped because Alan's dedication to a timeless spirit in dressing has kept his brand staunchly germane to menswear. Apart from the usual banking, legal, and corporate suspects, there's a new batch of entrepreneurs, tech billionaires, and creative professionals all seeking the kind of modern menswear that only Alan can provide. "Most people are probably unaware of how much more untraditional, off-beat, or high tech clothes we make. I work with so many fabric manufacturers who are willing to try something new if asked," Alan discloses. "It's just one of the many benefits of getting a custom made garment. We are able to undertake work that other brands won't or can't do."

One indication that Alan has never been moored to the past may surprise casual observers. Today, he willingly acknowledges a disinclination to wearing suits as often as he did in previous years. "Of course, I still do for some formal meetings," Alan clarified one blisteringly hot summer afternoon at the studio, as he sat back surrounded by the galleys of his book on Ralph Lauren that was soon going to press. To stress the importance of being comfortable in one's clothes, he gestured to what he was wearing: a white monogrammed shirt under what superficially appeared like a top-stitched denim jacket but was in fact made of soft linen. "I've been waiting forever for someone to come up with it, but no one did; so I had it made myself," he revealed, adding, "I just came back from Boston to see a Rolling Stones concert and I wore another version of this jacket there." Some may too quickly opine that Alan is beyond being beholden to appearing only in suits and ties surely. That may be so; but more to the point, Alan's sportier and relaxed look is in perfect accord with his adamant belief that menswear has to come as close to being a natural extension of the wearer as possible.

Alan attests that clothes may, and indeed ought to be, regarded as old friends. An inordinate amount of time is spent inhabiting them, after all. And like all old friends, they should be of the finest caliber and be treated as such. "Tweeds are exactly the kind of clothes that deserve that," he says. "Not only does tweed possess a unique allure and charm, it is the only garment that settles into you; and the more you wear it, the more it becomes a part of you." He recalls wearing tweed at an early age. "It was herringbone, probably a Brooks Brothers," he muses. But he's partial to another tweed garment he owns, an Italian-made tweed walking suit of a "loden hue and with two different colors along the large windowpane pattern".

Though he also commends tweed's adaptability both in rural and "quasi business" city settings, he admits finding little reason for its relevance to the average American. He concedes that its innate weight and density would normally be daunting to people who reside in warmer climates. Those in the American Northeast or in other cities where the seasons exert a palpable difference are far likelier to sport tweeds. But Alan, ever cognizant of the pragmatic aspects of clothing, bemoans how global warming has already shortened what used to be an October-to-March tweed season. Nonetheless, he contends that tweed's place in the pantheon of fine menswear is assured. "Yes, the well-traveled, more sophisticated dresser is the main market. But anyone with an interest in the best clothes will always gravitate toward tweed." Thus he regularly adds exclusively designed tweeds to his stock of woolens for the label. There are also archives of past designs that are still available to order. The lasting and ageless aspects of tweed are apposite to the "promise inherent in all Alan Flusser garments".

- - - - - - - -

That kind of assurance convinced Will to meet with Alan and Andrew at the designer's atelier to discuss his options. The primary decision at which they all arrived without hesitation was the creation of Will's tweed suit entirely in the house's aesthetic. Will says, "I wanted the suit to be an obviously Alan Flusser garment, cut in the manner synonymous with Alan's own classic taste, without compromising to today's prevailing fashions such as flat front trousers, narrow lapels, and overly slender silhouette." Will, of course, received the full Alan Flusser treatment. "This is a very collaborative process," Alan says. "If you're looking to get a tweed garment, I have to find out what part of the world you live in, where and how you plan on wearing it. For what purpose are you getting this suit? Is it for weekends in the country or moving around in the city? The answers directly tell me what weight the tweed should be, how it needs to be cut." And when choosing the cloth, Alan is also rigorous in selecting colors that complement the wearer's complexion.

For Will, another vital factor was the Alan Flusser made-to-measure services, which would get the suit made at a fraction of the cost of a bespoke garment. Will says, "Much as I wanted this suit, I could only commit absolutely to it so long as it wasn't just an unnecessarily exorbitant self-indulgence." To men for whom bespoke might be somewhat of a financial strain, getting suited in made-to-measure is inarguably the next best thing. At most shops that offer this service, it begins with the client trying on a sample suit within his size range. Someone, usually a tailor but not always, will then take his measurements specifically noting how much they digress from the standardized range of that prototype - accounting for body shape, jacket length or shoulder width.

Priced somewhere between bespoke and ready-to-wear, made-to-measure is now also available on Savile Row and from most major brands from Giorgio Armani and Prada to Paul Stuart and Joseph Abboud. There has also been a proliferation of men's labels that deal primarily in made-to-measure such as Artefact London, Beggars Run, and the still expanding Vancouver-based Indochino. Interestingly, while many stores have decamped for online retailing, Indochino began opening brick-and-mortar stores only after it had succeeded as a web-based brand launched in 2007. Left to one's own devices on its website, a customer would identify the standard size he wears and submit what can only be assumed are his proper dimensions. Still, the demand for better fitting suits prevailed over any fallibility in procuring suits online. Opening a physical store to support its e-commerce could be viewed as a canny maneuver. Indochino CEO, Drew Green, reveals that in cities where they do have brick and mortar stores, business has increased. The customers apparently appreciate how they can peruse the website first before making an appointment at the store to see and feel the merchandise. The success of this omni-channel model led Indochino to open its third New York store on Madison Avenue in 2018.

But not all made-to-measure suits are created equally. Each house (or brand) has its own criterion with regards to the number (around five is considered average) of adjustments it makes from the standard prototype. The more effort placed toward fairly negligible details like armhole size, the better the quality of the finished suit. Industry observers grant that computer aided design (CAD) has taken made-to-measure to as close to a bespoke level fit as it can get. While most of the suit, such as the main seam at the seat of the trousers, is still going to be machine finished, the reputable brands can at least be expected to have their own tailors and manufacturing facilities. They're also likelier to ring those bells and blow them whistles with more detailed hand finishing.

--- --- --- ---

In 2019, Paul Stuart launched its CustomLAB made-to-measure services, with the added option of custom dress shirts from Thomas Mason fabrics. Nestled in the same corner of Madison Avenue since it opened in 1938, Paul Stuart is named after founder Ralph Ostrove's (1899-1981) son, and was until recently a family-owned business. Universally believed to have been the first to roll out three-button, side vented jackets, Paul Stuart has existed for over eighty years without capitulating to fleeting fads. In 1955, Ostrove's son-in-law Clifford Grodd (1924-2010) took over as president and CEO. The company's longevity is mostly due to the firm hand (though some say it was more an iron fist) of former WWII military man Grodd, who burnished the brand image by streamlining the merchandise and adapting the logo of a man, book in hand, astride a split rail fence. That now recognized logo is said to be a representation of the fictitious character Dink Stover of Owen Johnson's "Stover at Yale", a novel about undergraduate life at the university during the turn of the 20th century. But the original 1921 illustration from which the logo is based was by Joseph Christian Leyendecker (1874-1951), the unrivaled American illustrator responsible for countless Saturday Evening Post magazine covers and the Arrow Collar Man ads.

After Grood died from cancer, the company was bought by its Japanese licensee Mitsui & Co in 2012. Thus far, it has continued to flourish by upholding its "craft of quarter inches" philosophy. The phrase refers to the precision of Paul Stuart standards when it comes to its wares - from the width of the ties to the spacing of the buttons. As an example, the long discontinued standard of half-sizes in ready-to-wear dress shirts and suits are still available here. But the same principle is as evident in the Paul Stuart style, which has remained an almost immovable standard bearer of quintessential American menswear for ages. Any concessions to shifting tastes, if any, were made in incremental and supremely subtle adjustments. A narrower lapel here, a tighter cut there. Because it never needed to be trendy or outré, Paul Stuart could always be counted on for dignified propriety.

For over ten years, the man responsible for ensuring the design reliability of the Paul Stuart brand is Ralph Auriemma. A soft spoken and unreasonably humble gentleman, Ralph says everything he knows about the business (and it is ample) he learned by lifelong hard work and on-the-job training. His steady climb from stock boy at a Brooklyn menswear store in the late 1970s to Paul Stuart creative director is archetypal New York a story if there ever was one. Raised by his grandparents in a typically stern Italian household, Ralph had teen indolence shocked out of his system when he was told in no uncertain terms to get a job or get out. He first found menial employment unloading bricks, which didn't last. He moved on and got a job at a local clothing shop where he was tasked with sweeping floors and re-stocking polyester shirts and flared trousers, dull chores which offered little by way of feeding his imagination. Yet in the long run, working there did.

Along the walls of the store hung photographs meant to persuade shoppers that they too could be this debonair if they had the sense to buy garments here. One in particular struck a chord in Ralph. It was a black and white 8 x 10 headshot of silent film star Ramón Novarro (1899-1968), Hollywood glamour personified in a suit and slicked back hair. "I'm not sure why, but somehow, I knew this was how I wanted to look," he discloses. "Right away, I had my 1970s shoulder length hair cut short. And because I had also started helping with sales, I began to wear a shirt and tie, and got myself a charcoal grey double-breasted suit." Needless to say, his new appearance impressed his employers and the customers. And that was merely the beginning.

"I began to watch more of those black and white movies that aired on late night television. I paid careful attention to the names in the credits of everyone who worked on the film from all the actors to who did the cinematography, costumes, or the scenery," he says. Of the many films he enjoyed dearly, he recalls some revered silent melodramas: "Flesh and the Devil" from 1926, "Love" from 1927, and "A Woman of Affairs" from 1928, all of which starred John Gilbert (1897-1936) and Greta Garbo (1905-1990), with costumes by Gilbert Clark (1883-), André-ani (1900-1953), and Adrian (1903-1959) respectively. Hollywood scuttlebutt has it because Miss Garbo's filmography consisted mostly of portraying mysterious women from *mitteleuropa*, for "A Woman of Affairs", Adrian was instructed by MGM mogul Louis B. Mayer (1884-1957) to make sure that her wardrobe in this picture was more befitting the role of a somewhat diffident rural Englishwoman. The legendary costume designer draped the actress in a mix of heavy pullovers and short tweed skirts. These celluloid fantasies and the people who made them were a source of endless fascination for Ralph. "This led me to buying books about the movies and the biographies of these talents - not just the larger-than-life personalities but the artists behind the cameras. I wanted to learn how they lived, how they thought, how they created. I was just so enamored of the era."

His infatuation with old Hollywood glamour would be one of arguably two factors that kicked off and dictated Ralph's aesthetic for the rest of his life. The other was triggered by his first trip into Manhattan. "One day, my boss took me with him to meet with suppliers," he recounts, "and suddenly I was in a brand new world of towering silver buildings with these masses of people, all well dressed in workday suits, rushing in all directions. It was all so breathtaking." He was hooked. Having seen what lay beyond the bridge, nothing could keep him from making a life there. The next two years were spent working tirelessly trying to escape Brooklyn. He offered to assist a road salesman and volunteered to schlep and sell sweaters to mid-Atlantic regional department stores. After several valiant attempts, he failed to make a single sale. But he did make enough of an impression with buyers and store owners to secure lasting contacts.

Then, he tore the back pages of a GQ magazine listing New York City menswear showrooms and systematically showed up at each one in hopes of getting a job. He found one place willing to take him on to tidy up after three salesmen. He was still performing the same stock boy duties, but he was in Manhattan at last. After months of pleading for a chance to try his hand at selling, the salesmen agreed to give him a break. He could try selling the lines during the weekends while the showroom was closed as long as he made sure to have everything back in readiness for Monday business. On Friday afternoons, he loaded up the garments into a car and drove to stores up and down the East Coast. He invariably came back on a Sunday night and made sure everything was clean, pressed, and returned on the racks. But this time, after each of these weekend trips, he came back bearing sales orders.

By his 20s, Ralph had his own apartment in a five-story Manhattan walk up on W89th. It wasn't the penthouse on Park Avenue he had seen in the movies but all that mattered was living in the city. And he was more than willing to take on whatever else was ahead of him. When a shirtmaker asked him to come up with a tie collection to complement his main line, Ralph wholeheartedly agreed to be sent off to Italy to meet with silk manufacturers. On the flight over to Europe, he was con-

vinced that all he had to do was find a reliable resource. To his dismay, when he finally found himself in front of one manufacturer after another, he realized how woefully unprepared he was in the rudiments of creating a collection. "I just didn't know a single thing about what I was doing," he says, looking back. The sheer variety of silks he had to sort through did nothing to mollify his anxiety. To his inexperienced eyes, as he kept shuffling through one swatch after another, they all began to blur together in an indistinguishable mass of colorful prints. It was at his very last meeting at a picturesque ruin of a villa on Lake Como that he felt his luck rebound. The proprietor led him into a cavernous room, a repository of generations of woven materials archived in dusty, leather-bound books. As he worked his way through decades of materials, he was inexorably drawn to those from the 1920s and 1930s. Once more, it was that old Hollywood look that captivated him. "I didn't know what I had been looking for in the first place, yet suddenly there it all was in front of me. Everything I could have ever wanted to make the tie collection," he says. He made his selections for samples to be made and sent to him in New York. After they later arrived, the shirtmaker hated them on sight. But Ralph stood his ground. And when the tie samples were shown alongside the shirts, all the buyers loved them. It would be the first but not the last instance that people would learn never to second-guess Ralph's taste.

He subsequently moved on to work with a couple of other brands, strengthening his credentials within the industry along the way. But it was an unexpected call from Jerry Lauren that took him on to the next important phase of his career. Jerry is, of course, the older brother of Ralph Lauren. He was the executive vice president and creative director for men's design at his brother's company and he was looking for someone to help develop fabrics for its new Purple Label. Ralph came highly recommended by the Italian factories he had worked with through the years and was summoned to a meeting with Jerry on a Friday morning.

Jerry liked what he saw of Ralph's work but told him he needed the other Ralph's final seal of approval to be hired. Jerry said he would be granted fifteen minutes to speak to Ralph Lauren. The two Ralphs wound up chatting for two whole hours. Ralph remembers it as an amiable conversation about shared interests. They talked of clothes and old movies, of Cary Grant and the New York Yankees. And by the end of it, Lauren asked when he could start. Ralph replied he needed two weeks to leave his current project. "No," countered Lauren. "I want you here Monday morning." And just like that Ralph would devote the next nine years of his life to Purple Label.

Like everyone who's ever worked there, Ralph admired the clarity and consistency of Lauren's vision for the brand. Ralph says that Lauren often said that it was never about "fashion", that instead he was "making a movie". The plot was the concept, whether it was sailing or equestrian. The soundstage was the setting of a shoot, whether it was the polo field or the drawing room of a grand house. Models were often given convoluted backstories about the "characters" they were playing in front of the camera. And it goes without saying, the wardrobe was very Ralph Lauren - style projected on a fantasy silver screen. Admittedly the ads and lookbooks that came out of these shoots do have the semblance of film stills, while others could've been plucked from out of the family scrapbook. The images shot for the Safari fragrance, for one, could be mistaken as scenes from James Hill's 1966 picture "Born Free". There's a photo of a guy in a tweed vest and plaid coat, walking down a dirt path with his dog that one may think was from someone's vacation. But, uh, isn't that Matt McColm? The guys hanging out on the lawn with the dogs look like friends who just finished a game of touch football. But that's Franz Holstaka at the center. And the guy in only his underwear lying back on a cot appears to be something from the North African desert campaign during the second world war. Pretty sure that's Doug Porter.

The Ralph Lauren brand celebrated its 50th anniversary in 2018. That's half a century of successfully repurposing traditional British dressing as an American dream lifestyle. Why, he practically invented this kind of cohesive lifestyle branding every other designer can only hope to emulate. And it seems almost scripted that Lauren, with his own matinee idol-like charisma, was first catapulted to stardom after being identified with a movie. In 1974, British film director Jack Clayton (1921-1995) brought to the screen the F. Scott Fitzgerald (1896-1940) literary classic "The Great Gatsby", starring Robert Redford as the titular Jay Gatsby. Although it received notices that were, to put it mildly, unkind, the film was moderately successful at the box office. Theoni V. Aldredge (1922-2011), who already had several theater awards to her name, nabbed that year's Academy Award in costume design for recreating hundreds of polished 1920s looks for the picture. She had designed suits and shirts for Redford and commissioned them from Lauren, whose on-screen credit solidified his brand image. Ralph Lauren the brand hit the peak of its leisurely stride across golf courses, tennis courts, and polo fields in the 1980s advocating power lunches in New York and summers in New England. Its Purple Label was the brand's move to upmarket ready-to-wear in 1994 with an approximation of the bespoke sensibility using fine quality garments made in Italy. In 2018 prices, a Purple Label men's suit would run around $1,500 to $2,000.

Ralph Auriemma says working at Purple Label was "the greatest experience of my career" and akin to a comprehensive masterclass in menswear. Part of his responsibilities there was putting together the concepts and fabrics. He would research the ideas and themes the team wanted to use and he then traveled to the major fabric exhibitions, trade shows, and mills to find the right materials. Usually, the fabrics were chosen only so far as how they could serve the season's overarching narrative. "But tweed was always on the list of what I had to find because it was a perennial staple at the company and it wasn't reliant on any trends," says Ralph. "We were all aware of the importance of the cloth in menswear and how it was integral to the brand."

Tweed, says Ralph, always had its own tales to tell. Once in 2000, Ralph found himself playing a starring role in one. After completing his meetings with fabric suppliers in Glasgow he took a spontaneous side trip to the Outer Hebrides. He recalls looking out the window of the small propeller plane he was on as it began its jittering descent toward Stornoway Airport. The sullen gray skies above the Isle of Lewis and Harris were quickly becoming inclement. Enormous waves hurtled to shore and exploded against the craggy coastline. Lightning flashed ahead the peals of distant thunder. The eight-seater twin-engine aircraft was being buffeted by turbulent winds and Ralph was white knuckling through the landing dressed in a turtleneck sweater over khaki jodhpurs, military boots, and topped off with a bomber jacket. Ralph couldn't help thinking how it was like he was in one of those motion pictures he loved so much. And the feeling lasted long after the plane had safely landed. His cinematic reverie continued to unspool throughout the rest of his stay on the island. He met with the local weavers who showed him how tweed was made. He spent quiet evenings at a quaint bed and breakfast in front of a roaring fire. He reminisces that when he later toured the shieling huts and moors, shrouded in mist and legend, "It felt like being transported to the past and setting foot on a sacred place."

After Ralph departed from Purple Label, he worked for a few years as creative director for various labels before hearing from a buyer in 2007 that Clifford Grood was looking for someone to hire at Paul Stuart. By then, Ralph's sterling bona fides left no room for doubt that he could get the position. It also helped that Grood was determined to attract a more youthful market with a new, separate line built around a fictitious persona who might represent that demographic. He just needed someone with Ralph's qualifications to see it all the way through from conception to delivery. And so Phineas Cole was born as the first ever new label for Paul Stuart and a way for the brand to have its cake and frosting too. Paul Stuart carries on, reputation unsullied; while Phineas gets to lark about, perhaps a tad more impulsive and spirited but no less lovable a scamp. Be assured: he may not truly break the rules but it's a fair wager he'll bend them a bit. And whatever mischief Phineas may be up to, it's all going to be done in good form.

With Phineas Cole, Ralph could skew the Paul Stuart aesthetic into more "experimental" directions. He began to tinker with the silhouette and added playful touches such as angled hacking pockets. And it was a near instantaneous hit, confirming Ralph's instinct that there was a market for a collection that reinterpreted and respected traditional looks simultaneously. In 2009, a 700 square-foot Phineas Cole boutique was installed in-store at Paul Stuart, the better to showcase this younger line of faultlessly tailored suits, cut leaner from an array of tweeds and other wool fabrics of more daring colors. A certified triumph was Ralph's Phineas Cole Fall 2012 collection. It featured Donegal tweed sport jackets, Shetland and lambswool three-piece suits of one-button jackets, flat front trousers, single or double-breasted waistcoats, lambswool and flannel Chesterfield coats. Outstanding details included button belt backs on coats and a wool shaft on a handsome pair of calf-skin shoes of Goodyear welt construction. Colors were also a highlight. One jacket with a matching vest was in blue-green checks. There were suits in red brick, aqua, and mauve. In a kind of subliminal messaging, one wool flannel coat had a Sherlock Holmesian detachable cape, while the shoot for that season's lookbook was styled with bowler hats (à la Patrick MacNee's (1922-2015) character John Steed, the British gentleman spy of the 1960s television series The Avengers).

Following several years of consistent sell-throughs and the Mitsui & Co buy-out, Ralph was officially named creative director in 2016. At his workspace in the warren-like maze of the Paul Stuart offices, he doesn't have a mood board. Rather, he has three wide mood walls, on which he continues to conjure cinematic expressions in design that he's dubbed "American sartorial" for both Paul Stuart and Phineas Cole. The differences between the two are understated and really more easily discerned by fashion experts. The more obvious ones lie in Ralph's fabric choices and how the garments are cut. He designs Paul Stuart and Phineas Cole with diligent dissimilitude while keeping both secured to the brand's signature style. This allows anyone to shop both lines, mix the items, and still achieve a cohesive appearance. It's a skill Ralph must have picked up during his tenure at Ralph Lauren where multiple product categories transit smoothly on separate orbits around Lauren himself. Though Ralph worked solely on Purple Label, he understood how each group is meant to serve the overall Ralph Lauren "lifestyle". According to Ralph, apart from Lauren, only a handful of people there had a better understanding of the nuances in every category than fashion illustrator Bill Rancitelli. Ralph raves, "Bill is among the most talented people I have ever met. His designs and illustrations were the backbone for many of the design teams at the brand."

- - - - - - - -

A highly regarded figure in New York's fashion community, Bill Rancitelli is a designer whose fashion illustrations are instantly recognizable works of art. Not only do his sketches so tacitly capture thematic purpose, but the models and garments are rendered with near photographic realism that they seem to move on the page. It's a talent developed during a lifetime dedicated to fashion. "When I was growing up I couldn't wait for the latest issues of Vogue and Seventeen to come out," he confesses. "I still have a complete collection of all issues of Vogue from the Diana Vreeland (1903-1989) era. I was just leafing through them the other day and found this layout with Ann Turkel wearing a one-shoulder tweed dress by Pauline Trigère!"

He reveals, "In junior high, I was already creating dresses. At school, we had a singing girl trio of one Polish and two Italian girls for whom I made very 1960s mod outfits." Bill went on to attend Parsons School of Design and after graduating, worked at such illustrious labels as Bill Blass and Anne Klein. In the 1970s, he was hired by Oleg Cassini to design his Munsingwear-manufactured tennis wear collection from New York. He was such an asset that when the head designer at the Oleg Cassini offices in Milan up and left with little notice, Bill was invited to take over.

Thus Bill relocated overseas, designed the main Oleg Cassini collection, learned the language, and for a while enjoyed, if not exactly *il dolce far niente*, at least the slower pace of Northern Italy. His work at Cassini was exemplary and life was good. But he eventually missed his wide circle of friends and the coruscating backdrop of the city too much. So after three years, he decided to return to New York and began what became a secondary career teaching design at his alma mater. At Parsons, Bill taught many budding talents who later became fashion stars such as Marc Jacobs, Isaac Mizrahi, Jack McCollough and Lazaro Hernandez, Mark Badgeley and James Mischka. On top of teaching, he worked with major designers like Norman Norell (1900-1972) and Halston (1932-1990).

Bill joined Ralph Lauren initially at Purple Label at its inception, almost at the same time as Ralph Auriemma. But Bill was only willing to sign up as a freelance consultant, a practice he prefers to this day. Within the company, his skills became much in-demand so he began working for its many divisions. Bill was at Ralph Lauren for sixteen years as a kind of session musician for different design orchestras. Several days a week he would float around the brand's many labels, designing and sketching a sundry of items. But to be clear, Bill was no mere pencil for hire. At Ralph Lauren, he designed knitwear, handbags, and footwear as well. In ways that cannot adequately be emphasized, it was Bill's fully-rendered collection presentations that were the most crucial. They served as the conduit by which the design teams and Lauren could reach visualized consensus. Bill very easily anticipated what Lauren wanted and any ambiguity of concept and mood were realized into certitude and unanimous agreement via his pencil and ink designs.

And did they keep Bill sketching. At any given moment, he would be asked to draw say twenty different glen plaid designs. He couldn't possibly recall anymore the number of tweed garments he sketched while he worked there. "We were trying to define an Americanized execution of traditional English tailoring," says Bill of those budding seasons at Purple Label. "It was wonderful drawing all those beautiful tweed outfits," he says. "I loved the dimensionality of how their base colors can gradate from light to dark." According to Bill, "For the collection, the obvious fabric choices we started out with were simply too hefty. It just made better sense to use Italian fabrics for a supple drape." Luckily for everyone at the brand, Bill knew full well how any specific fabric falls on the body and sketched each one accordingly. His artwork for the lighter Italian tweeds was so accurate they were compiled into the seasonal lookbooks that were sent out to buyers and press. Bill continued freelancing after leaving Lauren. Years later, he was contacted by another graduate of the Ralph Lauren finishing school of menswear, Joseph Abboud. Joseph wanted Bill to create artwork for his about-to-open flagship in 2014. For that commission, Bill drew seven 34" x 45" charcoal illustrations of original Joseph Abboud designs, which were then framed and mounted along a wall at the designer's Madison Avenue store.

- - - - - - - -

At Joseph Abboud's 1987 debut collection "An American at Oxford", the public witnessed a label that would use an international aperture through which American menswear could be refracted. And to this day that singular design sensibility has yet to be duplicated. Circumventing the slender-shouldered and wide-waisted suits of the time, Joseph offered a more sophisticated, natural silhouette, made visually compelling by unexpected colors and richer textures. His affinity for tweed was instantly apparent in the pheasant's eye patterned Shetland pieces, which also served as an opening salvo of what the label could accomplish with the cloth.

Joseph grew up in 1950s Boston, the adored youngest of four, and doted on by older sisters and loving parents. It would be remiss to overlook Joseph's Lebanese-American upbringing as a contributing component to his aesthetic; but it would be equally inaccurate to hang it all on a romanticized peg of exoticism. His creativity may have been enriched by his cultural heritage but it was fermented in Boston's intellectual setting. And it was further punctuated by the cultural references shared by all American kids of the era who were weaned on television and movies. He came to associate the clothes he saw in those larger-than-life projections as passports to otherworldly realities whether it was the evening jackets at Rick's Café Américain or a crofter's coat while trying to evade murderous spies on the Highland moors.

After studying comparative literature at the University of Massachusetts and French literature at the Sorbonne, Joseph received the offer of a teaching position at Brookline High School. He accepted the post, fancying himself in one of those tweed jackets with leather elbow patches he had seen so often at the movies. "The first one I owned though was a tan herringbone jacket of pure Scottish tweed," he says. "It was made in Paris by Pierre Cardin, with lavender stripes and cut with a continental flare." He purchased it in 1967 at Louis of Boston (the menswear emporium that opened in the 1930s and closed in 2015, a casualty of the current instability of brick-and-mortar retail and its own ill-advised move from Newbury Street to a waterfront building in South Boston). "I was spending so much money at the store back then I finally had to get a job there," he jokes about becoming a Louis of Boston buyer in 1968, and later director of merchandising until 1980. After a blink-and-miss-it stopover at Southwick clothing, he joined Ralph Lauren's Polo label and worked his way up to associate director of menswear design, a position he held until 1984.

The 1980s was a high point for Polo, and Joseph recalls many a time when the brand's conscientiously composed image bled into the everyday. When buyers (especially the out of town ones) had appointments at the showrooms, it wouldn't be entirely coincidental that Polo models would also happen to be around - like surfer Buzzy Kerbox wearing new Polo Shetlands or the Norwegian-born model Kristin Clotilde Darnell, known in the industry as simply Clotilde, in tartans. It was like coming to work and walking straight into a Slim Aarons photograph. One half expected to run into (Stephen) Laddie Sanford (1898-1977) in the hallways. Of course, twenty years later, the brand managed to sign an actual polo superstar in Argentine (Ignacio) "Nacho" Figueras as the "face" of Black Label and the various Polo fragrances. But it was always the movies that served as the most decisive source of inspiration to everyone at the brand. When Hugh Hudson's well-lauded 1981 picture "Chariots of Fire" came out, everyone who worked at Ralph Lauren went to see it. Joseph still remembers the tweed jackets and argyle sweaters in the film and says as British as they were, those garments also reminded him of the American preppiness of the Polo look.

It may very well be said that Joseph's tenure at these citadels of menswear honed his understanding of the business side of fashion, but he was always in possession of his own natural aptitude for style. During all the years he toiled within the clearly delineated bounds of those different brand images, Joseph always pushed for something more. He left Polo for attempts at launching his own label in ill-starred and quickly aborted alliances with rather dodgy entities. Fortunately, Guido Petruzzi (1934-2016) of Gruppo Finanziario Tessile (GFT) came along. GFT (Est. 1930) was an industry powerhouse responsible for manufacturing the biggest names in menswear such as Giorgio Armani and Valentino; and it was serious about adding the Joseph Abboud label to its roster

Joseph formed JA Apparel with GFT in 1988. And when he finally manifested the Joseph Abboud vision to the world, it was piquant with colors more lucent than were commonly utilized in menswear, and from fabrics profuse with surfaces that ripple to the touch. There were soft, glen plaid double-breasted suits and linen ties. The dress shirts had the British standard of omitting pockets, but the collection was still unmistakably American. Grounded as it was in classic tailoring techniques, the Joseph Abboud collection definitely had something fresh to offer: authority without being officious, relaxed without being static. Even in recline, the wearer is fully dynamic, ready to take on New York and the rest of the world. The industry was floored. That year, Joseph took home a Cutty Sark Award for Most Promising Menswear Designer. It was followed by consecutive Menswear Designer of the Year awards in 1989 and 1990 conferred to him by the Council of Fashion Designers of America. Season after season, Joseph found new ways to make suits that were less a man's outer garments, rather more like a part of his being.

In the 1990s, Joseph Abboud took its rightful place among the most coveted menswear lines in the market, branching out with an array of ancillary products including casual men's and women's wear. But when GFT began running into financial problems by decade's end, many of its labels began changing hands. Joseph sold his trademarks to new owners who, in turn, re-sold them to private equity firm J.W. Childs. Joseph tried to keep designing amidst the chaos but his dissatisfaction led him to step back. In 2012, he returned to the business as chief creative director at Tailored Brands, Inc. The following year, the company purposely acquired JA Holding Inc., the parent company that owns the Joseph Abboud label, in a deal which included the same New Bedford, Mass. factory that used to manufacture Joseph Abboud garments.

Joseph relaunched the Joseph Abboud designer collection under Tailored Brands Inc. in October 2014. The following year saw the opening of a 4,300 square-foot Madison Avenue Joseph Abboud flagship store, designed by Joseph in close collaboration with Jeffrey Hutchison & Associates, the design and architecture firm that specializes in fashion retail. The building's exterior was restored to a stone brown and adorned by elegant grey tweed awnings. Inside, the fifteen-foot vaulted, ivory Venetian plaster ceilings are supported by wood paneled square columns on which hang black and white publicity headshots of suave film stars including Cary Grant and Errol Flynn. On one wall are Bill Rancitelli's beautiful illustrations. Enveloping the space are wall coverings in grey Manila hemp, cream herringbone and taupe raw silk, along with gray washed oak, and bronze metal details. The main floor is illuminated by hand blown ovoid glass pendant lights with brass frames. An iron staircase dominates the space and leads up to the custom department where over two hundred fifty Italian fabric selections are on bronze hook displays. Clearly, having the brand and the designer who understands it best under the same roof has resulted in healthy growth for Tailored Brands. Having its own factory also generated a new revenue stream from the production of custom suits, sport coats, formal wear, and dress shirts under Joseph Abboud Black Label. Joseph says, "We now produce about 500 custom suits annually, a sure indication that there is a market for them."

Usually, the devoted tweed jacket client, says Joseph, will opt for custom over ready-to-wear. Either way, it all still begins with fabric. He says "It's the touch and feel of the material that decrees whether it should be a weekend sport coat or a formal jacket. And it's fascinating how the same pattern can look, fit, and feel so differently when you change the fabric." And that is why tweed will always be special, he says. Joseph has been consistently partial to colors derived from nature. He was once fixated by stones he picked from a beach that he hauled them in a bag through airport terminal checkpoints, then onto a shuttle all the way to Scotland where he showed them to mills and asked that they be translated into cloth. The mills, he says, are a constant joy to visit. "When I look through their big leather sample books full of wonderful swatches, I'm always amazed by the riot of colors, interesting patterns, and unique, not-so-safe stuff." Weeks later when swatches for his order from the mill arrived, he declares, "It was alchemy! The stones I had shown them had been turned to wool. Each yarn had been spun from twenty or thirty fine threads dyed in different shades. It took twelve colors to replicate the nuance of one tiny pebble.

"Tweeds are now being reinvented in lighter blends of wool, cotton, silk, and rayons. Herringbones, Donegals, barleycorns, pheasant's eyes and Russian twills are all vintage tweed patterns that I can make into soft jackets, sportswear vests, and casual pants," Joseph says. "They bring so many new options to a man's wardrobe where he can dress for a fall season with all the texture and character of tweeds yet be comfortable in almost any climate he lives in." And a typically cold day it was in February 2019 when Joseph's Fall collection was previewed for press and buyers at Pier 16 in South Street Seaport. From inside the makeshift plastic tent, passing ships were momentarily visible before melting away in the twilight. The choice wasn't arbitrary either since the collection was meant as a tribute to the immigrants who, from the 1700s through the 1800s, streamed through this very neighborhood after being cleared entry at Ellis Island. The models sauntering down a gangplank, however, looked less the huddled masses from steerage and more like they were stepping out of the covers of historic bodice rippers.

Of course, tweed had an earnest presence in the trend-defying collection of superb menswear. The jackets, trousers, capes, and coats communicated through unerring text and subtext the coming together of cultural influences. To those who aren't well-versed in the vernacular of runway presentations, the styling of the pieces, fabrics, accessories, and button or patchwork details may have been a confusing mix. But the initially uncomfortable conversation between elements, the clash of ideas, this is the catalyst to something new, better, and indeed more lavish. And that was the point Joseph wanted to make via his romanticized interpretation of the motley garments worn by early immigrants as they arrived with a farrago of value systems that inevitably coalesced into the rich tapestry that is now New York.

IV

❧

Here Today, Built to Last

When it came to choosing the particular tweed for his suit, Will unknowingly exhibited an affliction common to every true New Yorker: the conviction that 'good enough' is never good enough. But he had every reason to be circumspect. There would be no going back if the suit came out any less than what he had imagined. He did have specific thoughts on the matter, nevertheless. One had to do with checking out a small fabric company in London called Dashing Tweeds, which he heard had been doing some very innovative work with tweed.

And it so happened that Dashing Tweeds was just the kind of mom and pop business Will prefers to patronize as a way of "voting" with his dollar. "Nowadays, I do believe it's just become more important than ever to support small enterprises. Not only do they underpin the local economy, they come from a far more genuine place when it comes to the products and services they provide." As an added bonus, he says the fabrics created at Dashing Tweeds would be "impossible to find at ready-to-wear prices." Of the people behind Dashing Tweeds, Will says, "There's also much to admire about (founder) Guy Hills and what he's accomplished with cloth. There aren't many other manufacturers lately to have done more to push tweed into the future than he. I thought by buying from him, I could in a small way be a part of that."

- - - - - - - -

Tweed and the future have always been among Guy's consuming pre-occupations. A former freelance fashion photographer, he's a charming bespectacled chap with a buoyant demeanor. He has perhaps never been more aptly described than when *Primrose Hill* magazine's online social media editor Jason Pittock once wrote that being around Guy "is like being in the company of Caractacus Potts". Potts is, of course, the fictitious character created by Ian Fleming (1908-1964) author of the James Bond oeuvre. Though the name was slightly changed for the Roald Dahl scripted 1968 Ken Hughes (1922-2001) film version, Potts (portrayed by actor Dick Van Dyke) is the zany inventor who overhauls a dilapidated racing car into the flying Swiss army knife of a contraption called Chitty Chitty Bang Bang. And the comparison of Potts to Guy is uncannily on the nose. Guy has such an infectiously animated personality that he's practically a cartoon character. But this belies an astute intellect and inexhaustible creativity, which don't seem to come so much from any facility for design as sheer indomitable will. And for most of his life, Guy has channeled this bottomless wellspring of curiosity and ingenuity into his inventive and somewhat fantastical endeavors.

Guy's artistic aptitude may very well be regarded as a proud family tradition. He is the older of two sons born to an architect father and a journalist mother. His younger brother and a half brother are also architects. At one point, they lived in York House on Upper Montague Street where his father transformed the previously empty roof into a penthouse with a garden, and renovated the rest of the living quarters into a showplace with 1970s-era mirrors, brown diagonal striped carpets, and a cruciform column. Guy's grandfather was Dr. Elliot Philipp (1915-2010), the much respected obstetrician and gynecologist who wrote the groundbreaking 1939 book "The Technique of Sex" under the pen name Anthony Havil. Dr. Philipp's later work on in vitro fertilization with Dr. Patrick Steptoe (1913-1988) and Sir Robert Edwards (1925-2013) led to the births of the first so-called "test tube babies".

Dr. Philipp's wife Lucie Ruth Philipp (née Hackenbroch) originally of Frankfurt, Germany, was an affectionate Jewish grandmother and among Guy's formative influences. "They lived just around the corner on Harley House where my grandfather had his medical practice. On the way home from school, we'd always stop off there. Grandmother Lucie was German and would serve us scrumptious chocolate *lebkuchen* biscuits." But there was a catch. "She was such a stickler for good manners and punctuality that we absolutely had to be there on time, or we wouldn't get any *lebkuchen*." Her husband had been a well-traveled man who had accumulated an impressive art collection and she was only too willing to inculcate an appreciation for the arts in her grandchildren. Guy recalls, "She talked about art often. She was also very proud of her collection of snuff boxes and beautiful antiques. And oh how she loved opera! My best memories of her include days of seeing her so beautifully dressed in tweed suits, all made for her by a tailor. She used to take me along for shopping trips to choose the fabrics for her dresses at John Lewis (the high-end department store). As a child, I was dazzled by those bolts of colorful fabrics they had stacked all the way up to the ceiling."

Making even a mundane outing into something of a rollicking adventure is a penchant of Guy's. One day, he took one of his grandfather's discarded Gold Block pipe tobacco tin cans from Ogden's of Liverpool and used it as a rudimentary survival kit. He recalls laughing, "I had matches and some potassium permanganate so I could start a fire, a mirror, magnifying glass, and fish hooks and wire for fishing. I think it was from reading Robinson Crusoe once too often!" He then reasoned that should some mishap leave him stranded on a deserted island, it would probably be beneficial to know how to make his own clothes. So he asked his grandmother Lucie to teach him how to crochet. Guy became engrossed by the mechanics of crocheting. "I was so intrigued by how all these rapid and repetitive movements could create something," he says. Though he concedes never having knitted more than crochet caps, the experience would set into a pattern of behavior in which Guy would fixate on something and he would be determined to figure out the nuts and bolts of how it's done.

While he was attending Westminster School, established by Bene-dictine monks as far back as the fourteenth century, Guy discovered photography. He had always seen his mother go on reporting assign-ments with a photographer in tow. But after she got her own Canon A-1 camera, Guy took every opportunity to borrow it. Long before the "selfie", Guy was his own test subject. With camera held by an out-stretched arm and strategically placed mirrors, he familiarized himself with how to use angles and light. And no one else in the household was spared from being photographed in an endless variety of poses - not his parents, not his brother, not even the family dog.

It was also then that he happened to catch a special showing of Michelangelo Antonioni's (1912-2007) 1966 thriller "Blow-Up" at the city-funded Barbican arts centre. With nary a second thought, Guy de-cided the glamorous milieu of the highly influential motion picture, though set decades prior, was exactly where he belonged. In the picture, a London fashion photographer (played by actor David Hemmings, 1941-2003) allegedly a celluloid simulacrum of David Bailey, was con-stantly surrounded by beautiful women like Vanessa Redgrave, Jane Birkin, and the Countess Vera von Lehndorff-Steinort (the model known to the fashion industry as Veruschka). "I told myself this was the life for me," Guy attests. He embarked on his budding career in photog-raphy by turning a spare bathroom at home into a dark room, which was soon littered by trays of processing chemicals and drying portraits hanging on a clothesline. Unbeknownst to him, his mother was ac-quainted with photographer and filmmaker Antony Charles Robert Armstrong-Jones (1930-2017), the 1st Earl of Snowdon, more commonly referred to as "Lord Snowdon". She had been showing Guy's pho-tographs to Lord Snowdon who advised her, "He has to get himself a medium format camera."

After Guy did get what he calls a "proper camera", he won an award for his photographs as part of an initiative by a youth-dedicated charity formed out of the Fairbridge Society, founded by Kingsley Ogilvie Fair-bridge (1885-1924). Some of Guy's winning photos, snapshots of Lon-don and school life, accompanied the feature story on the awards in The

Times. The "prize" was a working trip to a sheep farm outside of Perth in Australia. He recalls, "When I got there, I was just awestruck by how contrary it was from London with all the wide stretches of land and sunny skies." Toiling for three straight months at the farm, Guy learned everything about tending to sheep from feeding and herding to shearing them. Little did he know back then, of course, how important wool would later become for the rest of his life.

When he returned to London, Guy went to Bristol University (Est. 1595) to study Biology. He says the course aroused his interest in the inner structure of things and how different parts connect with each other in order to function. Before going off to university though, he confesses, "I took one of my father's Harris Tweed jackets with me. I don't recall asking his permission. I just pulled it from his closet and packed it. He hardly wore it so I probably thought he wouldn't mind." Looking back on why he picked that particular jacket, he says, "Its herringbone pattern gave it a gentlemanly quality that I thought made me look more grown up." A definite plus was how he thought wearing the jacket made him appear like "a Victorian scholar or an adventurer". While he thought then that it fit him well, he realizes now, "I had good shoulders and in those days a trimmer waist so the jacket was a little too big for my frame." Nonetheless, he says "I loved its ruggedness and shape and these details like the ticket pocket, which I found appealingly old fashioned. It also had a huge 'poachers' pocket inside which was very useful for stuffing things. It felt like a proper piece of clothing; though the reddish brown color made it nothing like a formal suit or my school uniform. I put it on and just never took it off. Several nights, I definitely fell asleep in it. And I still have it today."

But at school, too many things were vying for his attention that Biology naturally fell by the wayside. "I was far more interested in going to parties and taking pictures to pay heed to school work," he says. "It was also then I met my future wife Natasha. I was immediately entranced. She was tall and beautiful. And of course I thought she was way out of my league." While Guy readily admits to not being part of the popular crowd, his photography, not to mention his naturally jovial nature, did endear him to most of the other students. After his parents divorced, his father went on to remarry a woman who was in the dress business. Guy turned to her to learn something different. He wanted her to teach him how to sew. And like most everything else he's ever attempted, learn it he did. Practicing his newly acquired skill on a Bernina sewing machine he made himself a T-shirt and patched up some of his torn jeans. He subsequently learned more complicated techniques like how to French seam and craft outrageous outfits for going to raves.

When the 1990s rave scene was at full bore, the clubs of choice for acid house fans were the Haçienda and the Mud Club at Bagley's Warehouse. If they were otherwise too packed there were always several other underground parties going on at open fields, empty parking lots, warehouses, and at the estates of young toffs. Guy invariably showed up at these parties in his DIY costumes, each more outlandish than the next. Straight out of a Charlie Brown newspaper strip was this kite outfit, comprised of enormous nylon triangles that reached down to his feet and an extended tail. There was a gold Lurex jumpsuit with epaulets. Once, he sewed a 20 foot-long caterpillar outfit into which he and his friends huddled to form a gyrating green train with fluffy green feet. And there were hats, lots of them, usually fluorescent and equipped with ping pong balls or some other wacky surprises. It's a wonder how Guy ever made it to graduation. Somehow he managed. "Upon graduation, I started working as a photo assistant to various photographers in London," he recounts. When he was able to eventually strike out on his own, he shot for a handful of teen magazines. He was later upgraded to doing hyper-saturated fashion layouts for glitzier books like Country Life and Tatler, affording him a London studio of his own with a darkroom that didn't have to double as a loo.

And so his fantasy "Blow-Up" life of shooting glamorous models all day long had come true. As his career advanced, so too did his man-about-town creds. He was dating. But at that point Natasha was the proverbial one that got away. "I was pining for her," Guy sighs. "We still ran into each other regularly at parties when she was a promising young lawyer." On one such chance encounter, he finally mustered up the nerve to ask her out. To his surprise, she relented. They started see-ing each other regularly but whether imagined or not, Guy suspected Natasha was unconvinced of his sincerity. Photographers aren't really known for leading the life of celibate monks. "She was always at my flat but she never left a single thing behind," he laughs. "So, on a ski trip in Switzerland I pulled out my mum's ring from my pocket and proposed." They were walking along a lovely park. He was on tenter-hooks and kept vacillating. "It was such a beautiful setting, you know, the trees, the snow. And I was so nervous I kept changing my mind about how this spot was perfect, and then, oh no that one over there is better." But when he finally popped the question? Crickets. She needed time to think. So Guy grudgingly waited a few weeks longer for the happy outcome that took place when they were back in London. They married at a church in Kensington. And never mind the bride, everyone wondered what Guy would wear. Much to the amazement of many in attendance, Guy showed up wearing a flawless but most conventional morning dress with top hat. "I believe in dressing for the occasion," he says. "My best man cracked a joke during his speech, something to the effect of how relieved everyone was I didn't show up in some nutter out-fit."

In 2004, Guy was assigned by a magazine to shoot portraits of tailors on Savile Row. There, he ran into an old friend from university, An-drew Bolton, currently the head curator of the Metropolitan Museum of Art's Costume Institute in New York. As luck would have it, Bolton told him that the Savile Row Bespoke Association (SRBA) had recently been formed and the group was looking for a photographer to shoot im-ages for its campaigns. The SRBA is a non-profit marketing cooperative set up to consolidate Savile Row's houses in promoting the bespoke in-dustry. Bolton passed Guy's name along to Anda Rowland of (one of the row's premiere shops Anderson & Sheppard and) the SRBA. "I leapt at the chance," Guy says. "For over four years thereafter, I was pretty much just shooting for Savile Row." The steady job also relieved him of having to travel constantly for gigs and allowed him to settle down and start a family, which today includes wife Natasha, three children, Amelia, Hector, Rex, and a dog called George.

Guy really enjoyed photographing and getting to know the different houses on the row. The tailors' fabric archives were of particular interest to him. For his work with the SRBA, Guy hit on the idea of bartering his photography services for tailoring. "I must have gotten a suit from almost every tailor at Savile Row." The problem was he says, "All the new fabrics were so boring. I was always looking for something more daring and stylish." It was at a showing of the masters collections at the Royal College of Art where Guy stumbled into what he sought in the work of a talented fabric designer called Kirsty McDougall, who perhaps not coincidentally originally hailed from the Outer Hebrides.

- - - - - - - -

Kirsty was born in Lewis, but at age six, she and her parents moved to Perthshire. "We moved for my parents' work as teachers. But we did return regularly for summer holidays on the island," she says. She recollects those long lazy days fondly, visiting friends, walking to old haunts, swimming at the beaches, or sitting beside the local weavers, spellbound by how they loomed Harris Tweed. "I've always been creative," she says. "My father tells this story of how when I was very young he would watch me dropping stones and flowers into a water barrel to create patterns." At ten she had a notebook filled to overflowing with ideas, design sketches, and fabric choices for her very own fashion house. Although she discovered other interests as she grew up, she never stopped imagining and drawing. She consequently matriculated to Dundee's Duncan of Jordanstone College of Art & Design (origins dating back to 1881) where she earned a Bachelor of Arts degree in constructed textiles. The experience formalized her understanding of design, tempering her creative impulses with direction and rationality. School, she says, gave her "a better appreciation for being more analytical and for creating an end product, things that serve a practical purpose. I learned how to be less self-indulgent when designing." And like all young people on the cusp of adulthood, the experience also sparked her desire to move beyond the borders of where she grew up and be "at the center of things", which to her meant London. So, she applied to get her masters at the Royal College of Art (Est. 1837) in South Kensington, the only entirely postgraduate art and design university in existence.

The collection Kirsty presented for her masters in constructed textiles consisted of woolens, silks, and cottons, as well as finished women's garments. It was a perspicacious study on the polarity of taste all the while implying that there is no such thing as good or bad ones. "It was a very surreal installation," she says, "rooted in the punk movement." She highlighted tweed's tangible coarseness as emblematic of innocence, superimposing graphics over them to deconstruct and subvert its perceived classicism. But surpassing the ideas, it was their implementation that tantalized Guy. The tweeds were truculent without being obnoxious and Guy saw in them glimmerings of Vivienne Westwood. He gushes, "I've always been a fan of Westwood and used to buy some vintage pieces of hers from a dealer in Notting Hill Gate. I once went to Christie's to bid for some!"

Kirsty wasn't at the presentation on the day Guy came to see her collection so he left a message asking to meet with her. "Once we did, we got along, and I started working with him by styling for his shoots," she says. About a month later, he broached the subject of possibly having her design some wovens for him. Guy says, "That collection of hers somehow stayed with me and I thought maybe she could make something for me. But, she knew nothing about actual fabric production. After some research she found a yarn supplier and a commission weaver in Scotland who completed the cloth for us." Guy loved the result she delivered. But he only needed 10 of the minimum order of 60 meters to get a suit made for himself. Left with an excess of 50 meters, Guy says, "I already had my beautiful suit from the original design. So I decided I could just try and sell what was left over. From there, the plan then escalated to making this an ongoing enterprise. I could ask Kirsty for more designs and whatever I couldn't use, I would sell."

Guy was also sensing that digital was about to change photography as he knew it. He thought he had better start looking for something else on which to fall back, just in case. He says, "With a family to support I had to seriously figure out what other things I could do that didn't involve a piecemeal kind of existence. The more I thought about it, the more I became convinced I could make selling Kirsty's tweeds into a business." Similarly, Kirsty was at a crossroads with regards to work. He says, "So I suggested we get a design loom and set up a studio." And of course it was all going to be about tweed. At first blush, Guy's idea unavoidably came across as, to use the clinical parlance, "bonkers". "I was sitting there and thinking that no way this was going to happen," says Kirsty. But she listened. And she heard. "Guy is so persuasively enthusiastic about what he believes in that you can't help but get swept along," she laughs. Moreover, there was something about offering tweed as something radically different and yet not that spoke to her. What began as an isolated request to get a unique suit made was fast developing into something far more complicated and life-altering than either of them could ever have anticipated.

"I bike around town a lot," Guy says. "And my wife's always asking why I don't wear one of those horrible reflective tabards for safety. Then I thought, maybe I could have a decent looking outfit made of tweed with a modern function. I quickly realized it could be the start of potentially giving men wider fabric choices of unlimited color and texture for varied garments. And it wasn't going to be some half-hearted 'classic with a twist' nonsense - but a whole new concept in tailored menswear. I gradually became more resolute about this idea of taking tweed's heritage and modernizing it with unabashedly directional patterns, a way of bringing it into the urban environment. Tweed is already an ideal matrix for integrating technical yarns such as reflective threads. It could then become the basis for updating traditional British-tailored sportswear with all these burgeoning materials and tech."

At Kirsty's apartment in Hackney, where she still lives today, she and Guy set up, ad hoc, a studio with an arm loom for making prototypes. There, they dreamed up the name Dashing Tweeds, co-opting the word "dashing" and its allusions to both looking debonair and darting ahead. "We contacted mill after mill, manufacturer after manufacturer," says Kirsty. But none of them were exactly falling all over themselves to take part in the plans of the duo. "They weren't about to listen to a couple of amateurs who didn't know what they were talking about, much less guarantee minimums or consistent orders." As usual Guy was undeterred. They persisted until they landed on the doorstep of Robbie Trussler and Drove Weaving. Kirsty says they were lucky, "Robbie said he'd give it a go because he liked a challenge." Guy chimes in, "He saw straight away that Kirsty is very talented and experiments with structures that are very rarely used. It's never just bosh off something easy for the weavers." Robbie admits there was nothing easy about making the tweeds for Guy and Kirsty while, for the most part, other companies only need the types of work where "it's just following on".

Guy's requirements, on the other hand, were uncommon and expensive. The cheaper companies may want "miles of stuff", but Robbie says he's not in the game to compete with the big guns as far as mass production goes. He's more interested in the one-off, the quality, the luxury. "Robbie didn't blink an eyelid when we asked him to experiment with the reflective yarn. And we've since sent over some pretty crazy designs," Guy says. According to Robbie, Guy is the only person for whom he'd done this kind of work. The finished product is Dashing Tweeds "Lumatwill" cloth, embedded with luminescent fibers by 3M called Scotchlite and made into "Retroglo" yarn by the Metlon Corporation, and waterproofed by Schofield Dyers and Finishers. Robbie suspects that someone down the line will try but would no doubt find it impossible to mass produce the same styles.

After the production of a handful of patterns, Dashing Tweeds was ready to, well, dash. When a commercial space opened up at the end of Savile Row, on Sackville Street, Guy leased it and moved right in. He thought that being in the immediate vicinity of the row would burnish the reputation of his fledgling shop with that of the neighborhood's. He also accounted for the convenience of having his cloth readily available to the tailors on short notice. It would be expedient as well to send Dashing Tweeds customers over to any of the next door neighbors for tailoring. He was already well acquainted with all their specific house styles, besides.

"The place used to be a hair salon and they had left behind some of their fixtures," he says of the Sackville Street location. "I was completely clueless about retail so I just came in with buckets of paint ready to spruce up the space. But I was then told I needed to submit renovation blueprints to the building landlord for approval before I could start any kind of work." He complied, being all too aware how important it was for them to have a physical store. He says, "We needed a real shop because cloth is all about touch. Tweed in particular has to be felt." To ready the store, he also began creating off-the-peg jackets, which were as much for himself as they were depictions of what customers could get at Dashing Tweeds. Trouble was, most of these were designed with a trifle more flair than might be comprehensible to the average customer. "In the early days I worked with fashion students making all sorts of things such as circularly cut cycle trousers and jackets based on 16th century armors." Clearly the ancient proverb "Don't get high on your own supply" was unknown to Guy. He laughingly adds, "I made things I wanted, thinking everyone else would want them too. The main learning curve was understanding I needed to make things that actually appealed to others as well."

Guy abandoned his more histrionic flights of fancy and prudently focused on making modernly functional tweeds. "We try to think about how people live today from jumping on a bike to working out or traveling across the world. And we imagine ways for everyone to look spruced up while they're doing those things. We're not interested in just recoloring old designs. Rather than look back to an era and romanticizing a way of life that may or may not have existed, we want to look ahead." Still, lest people assume Guy has lost his sense of romantic drama, let it be known that Dashing Tweeds officially markets itself to the "modern urban knight".

- - - - - - - - -

In 2018, Dashing Tweeds moved to a more commodious space at 47 Dorset, just north of Mayfair. Luxury pulses steadfastly through the veins of this London neighborhood. But while its central street, New Bond, pounds on the unchecked ostentation of logo-centric labels and arrivistes, Dashing Tweeds aims at bridging the needs of flashier customers with those from back on Savile Row. At Guy's old stomping grounds, heritage brands still insist on proceeding at a pace of civilized decorum. And the less said of the nearby Abercrombie and Fitch store the better.

Savile Row is the undisputed world capital of bespoke men's suiting. The Old English verb "bespeak" birthed "bespoke" in reference to goods that were "spoken for" or have been ordered. Today, a bespoke suit typically starts at around £5,000, takes on average a twelve week minimum to arrange, and requires some sixty hours of precise tailoring. Buttonholes, padding, and stitching are all done by hand. Machinery is used only to ensure the sturdiness of pockets, center back, and side seams. Haste is nothing but a nuisance here and discreetly brushed aside like lint on one's shoulder.

Everything moves along with an almost ceremonial cadence - from the instant the bell over the door announces an arrival to the taking of painstaking measurements, from picking out the desired cloth all the way to the final fitting. One tarries over the fabric selections and engages in conversation about *divertissements*. One hesitates about the width of the lapels or frets about how snug the jacket should feel. Does one indulge in some padding or go *spalla camicia*? Forging a rapport with the house cutter is also vital. The totality of the experience is what bestows ultimate personalization on the suit. Though a bespoke suit is obviously crafted to specifications, each of the shops on the row boasts its own signature cut. A familiarity with those is strongly advised before patronizing a particular establishment.

Tailors first opened businesses in the area sometime in the late 18th century on Cork Street before settling on Savile Row by 1803. And much that has changed in the intervening years is as much as what has remained the same. On this street are several fabled names. There's

Dege & Skinner (Est. 1865) and Henry Poole & Co (Est. 1806), the last two family-run businesses. Dege & Skinner at No. 10 has been granted three royal warrants and introduced tailor-made shirts as part of its regular wares. Henry Poole & Co at No. 15 holds several royal warrants and reportedly created the precursor to the American tuxedo. However, where once the row was patronized predominantly by those for whom the old fashioned and only acceptable way to make money was by inheriting it; these days, efforts have been exerted to attract a more democratic array of customers.

"We're not interested in being preserved in aspic," declares Patrick Grant, managing director of Norton & Sons located at No. 16. Not that the house doesn't have its own storied past. Founded by Walter Charles Norton in 1821, its original location on the Strand allowed it to cater to the city's working class men; and given the proximity to Fleet Street, that probably included many an ink-stained journalist. Its growing business in the 1850s supported a move to bigger accommodations on Conduit Street where it cultivated both a tonier clientele as well as stronger ties to the more leisurely sporting activities. A decade later, Norton & Sons finally arrived at No. 16 Savile Row where it was conspicuously dwarfed by its neighbors in terms of production output because it was only capable of employing seven tailors and two cutters at a time. None of this, however, dissuaded several members of European royalty and American presidents from becoming fervent patrons.

If ever there was a face of the latter-day Savile Row it is Patrick's. He acquired Norton & Sons in 2005. All these years later, this material and science engineering degree holder and Oxford MBA candidate still cuts the kind of figure of someone who seems more likely to be standing in front of a three-paneled mirror at the tailor's rather than manning the place. But when first he heard that Norton & Sons was on the block, the prospect of reviving such an esteemed brand was too enticing to ignore. In Patrick's estimation, somewhere along the way, the previous owner had allowed the house to veer off the rails and stoop to primarily peddling hunting and fishing gear. By his reckoning, all it really needed was a course correction to steer it back toward profitability. So certain was he in its eventual feasibility he reveals, "I sold my house and car to raise money to buy the place." He was also able to coax others - including his grandmother, a friend from prep school, and even a mate who was a year behind him at Oxford - to invest in his venture.

To Norton & Sons, Patrick administered some "love and attention". Under his helm, the house narrowed its sights on furnishing fine menswear along with dispensing the faultless personal service for which Savile Row is known. One particular perk for American clients was the revival of the house's tradition of traveling to the US yearly to meet with them. Although started at Norton & Sons in the 1970s by then-owner and seasoned Savile Row tailor, John Arthur Granger (1933-2018), this service was already being extended a decade earlier by other tailors to their clients who resided as far away as Los Angeles. Now, menswear brands from Italy (such as Pomella, Ambrosi, Liverano & Liverano, Sartoria Solito, Dalcuore), France (Cifonelli), and Japan (Caid) also regularly dispatch tailors to meet with overseas clients. Some have shrewdly coordinated their trips and shared showrooms from which to operate.

- - - - - - - -

In 2019, Norton & Sons' head cutter Nicholas Hammond welcomed CEOs, lawyers, architects, and financiers to a spacious-for-New-York though still understated hotel room in midtown. On a table were needle and thread, a pair of scissors, pattern paper, and chalk embossed with the Norton & Sons shield. In a three-piece suit with tape measure at the ready, Nicholas stood knee deep in swatches, samples of ties, and pocket squares, looking every bit the seasoned cutter. Still, there will be some who may think he looks awfully young to be one, facial hair aside. Relative to other houses, he may well be, but this has also helped Norton & Sons appeal to younger customers who might be more amenable to current style advice from someone closer to their own age.

Nicholas has worked in the garment trade prior as a merchandiser for UK retailer Reiss and the Spanish brand Zara. He had also taken a basic tailoring course at Newham College. He landed his apprenticeship at Norton & Sons in 2011 and worked his way up to being appointed head cutter in 2016. He does recall some push back in the early years when more than a few customers greeted his youth with a wary countenance. In time though, the poise with which he dealt with them won over the most obdurate skeptics. In his capacity as cutter he is part tailor, part psychiatrist, part father confessor to these clients.

Possibly the easiest aspect of the job is assessing someone's physical dimensions. To a trained person, a cursory glance is all it takes; otherwise that's why there's a tape measure. As anyone who's ever worked in retail can attest, it's what the customer wants that's always the conundrum. There are often enough people who don't know what they want. But even those who are sure they do may not be able to quite convey it. Worse still are those whose choices are flat out wrong. So, Nicholas has to tread carefully, listen attentively to the client's wishes, and hopefully intuit the right course of action. He asks questions about how or when the client intends to wear the suit. Should it be necessary, he will probe further into their work or pastimes as they are pertinent to the suit. And he will provide a sympathetic guiding hand throughout the process.

Moreover, as head cutter, Nicholas is also responsible for making sure all of Norton & Sons' moving parts are running in unison. "We're a very small house," Nicholas points out. "So part of what I do is keep everyone on track, like letting our staff know who is coming in that day or when a certain garment has to be ready. But mostly I'm involved with the fittings, taking garments apart, re-cutting the paper patterns, re-cutting the actual garments, then handing them over to the tailor with any necessary notations on what has to be done."

- - - - - - - -

The addition of Nicholas to his team has enabled Patrick to take on more ambitious endeavors through the years, such as rescuing other fixer-upper fashion companies. In 2009, it was E. Tautz (founded by

Edward Tautz in 1867), the brand credited for the 'Knickerbocker' breeches as well as for crafting sporting clothes in waterproof tweeds and meltons. "More directional chic menswear" is how Patrick describes his revived E. Tautz line with its generously cut silhouettes and styling leavened by a droll British sense of humor. It earned him a Menswear Designer award at the British Fashion Awards in 2010. This was followed by his 2013 relaunch of sportswear label Hammond & Co (founded by Robert Hammond in 1876) in collaboration with retailer Debenhams (Est. 1778) as high street and casual ready-to-wear line at accessible prices.

Of course, rebuilding these brands took some doing. But for someone who freely professes to having had no previous experience in the industry, Patrick's not doing shabbily. Bolstered by his affability and photogenic looks, he's also gained an authoritative patina (and adoring fans) via starring as a "celebrity" judge on the telly's "The Great British Sewing Bee", a reality show with amateur contestants jostling for the honor of being "Britain's best home sewer". (And yes, someone on that production should've rethought that title.) But stepping into the rag trade wasn't altogether the initially assumed hard pivot for the entrepreneur. To begin with, he already had more than a nodding acquaintance with the lifestyle represented by these brands. And while he knows the labels he's taken on well enough to differentiate them from each other, he also abides by a set of cardinal principles that inform everything he does with all of them. "I've always believed that simple is better," he states to explain why he eschews any unnecessary details in the garments. "That's why it's all the more important that we get the details quite right. We avoid loads of guff so we have more money to spend on the actual material like Harris Tweed for the hats or on Baird McNutt linens for our summer pieces."

- - - - - - - - -

Just before Nicholas landed in New York, Norton & Sons was approached, along with the other houses, to help promote the row in conjunction with the popular Chelsea Flower Show. The activation, in collaboration with Flowerbx, was dubbed "Savile Row in Bloom" and ran for five days in May 2019. Allegedly, each shop was asked to select a specific cloth to represent the house. They were informed that these would then be rendered in flowers to be displayed in front of their respective windows. The Norton & Sons people heartily chose tweed as their fabric. Word of the project got around and was greeted with much excitement. Oddly though, when the flowers arrived, they were the same arrangements for all the houses. What might have been may be open to conjecture, but one can more or less suppose what in fact happened. Perhaps, they were simply unable to create the appropriate arrangements on schedule. Or, more probably, the florists belatedly discovered that translating different fabrics into flora was an unrealistic undertaking. Without that translation though, an implied connection between flowers and tailoring strains credulity, catchy titles notwithstanding.

Patrick only learned of the matter after the fact. Still, it didn't surprise him that his Norton & Sons staff would pick tweed. Everyone who knows him is aware of his being an outspoken advocate of tweed for both professional and personal reasons. Edinburgh born and raised, Patrick's been wearing tweeds most of his life, from the hand-me-downs he got from his father and grandfather to his green Harris Tweed school uniforms. He remembers with amusement many rainy days of his youth boarding a public school bus reeking like a soaked canine, packed as it was with kids marinating in tweeds. "All those uniforms were second or third hand, by the way, and they were still in excellent state" he says to underscore the fabric's resilience. He would even hazard a guess that his is still being worn today by another student. And Patrick harbors no qualms over being clad in previously worn garments, so long as they're well made, but of course. "We have an American customer who recently came in with two original Norton & Sons tweed suits from the 1950s. They were his dad's and he wanted them recut to his measurements." Patrick is confident said gentleman will be served well by those suits for another twenty years.

Tweed occupies a more meaningful place in Patrick's personal convictions with regards to the business of fashion itself. "Tweed, and authentic Harris Tweed specifically, has the smallest carbon footprint in making clothes," he avers. "We need to seriously reevaluate how we shop. Clothes should be something you enjoy and cherish. The accelerated consumption of cheap, disposable clothing is not only damaging to the economy but has a lasting, ruinous impact on the planet." His insistence seems rather impolitic from someone of his stature in an industry propelled by obsolescence. Yet it is hardly tendentious reasoning and has less to do with not buying clothes rather being mindful of what one does buy. His view of this moral imperative is echoing among young people who are becoming more informed about the encroaching effects of climate change. He says people aren't doing themselves, nor the world, any favors by the cavalier stockpiling of clothing, especially ones of inferior virtues.

The mass market category called "fast fashion" became a thing in the 2000s as a response to the demand for more, cheaper, and available pronto merchandise. Expeditious manufacturing capabilities and low cost labor by disadvantaged populations led to a glut of garment companies shamelessly ingratiating themselves to millennials with shaky loyalties. Though it has its detractors, fast fashion is also obviously a business model congruent with marketing to an entire generation conditioned to subsist on a steady diet of downloadable gratification and Instagram likes. Never mind that the clothes have all the structural integrity of a wet paper bag. Still, there may yet be light on the right swipe.

"Twenty years ago, nobody thought about the environmental consequences of this; but today's generation has grown up being aware of how disposable plastics are polluting our oceans." He says, "An estimated 15-25% of all ocean plastic can be traced back to discarded polyester fiber from clothing that doesn't biodegrade. That's millions of tons of plastic going into the sea just from washing cheap clothes!" He raises an equally compelling case for swinging the pendulum back to people caring more about where and how the clothes they purchase are made.

"Fortunately, interest in ethically made and sustainable fashion is gaining steam," he points out. He's of the reasonable opinion that no one would consciously want to be party to enabling brands that pollute the environment or outsource labor to impoverished people being kept in indentured servitude.

Patrick's crusade for the industry's (as well as the planet's) long-term survival has also taken other forms. In 2015, he bought Cookson and Clegg (Est. 1860), a manufacturing supplier for E. Tautz, in what some industry cynics criticized as a "sentimental" attempt to keep it afloat. Unfortunately, a year later it still sank, as a result of a far too familiar plight among factories reliant on the feast or famine of seasonal fashion manufacturing. These companies often oscillate between operating at full capacity and having no work at all, a precarious way of doing business known only too well by every tweed weaver in the trade. In hopes of alleviating the situation, while supporting the local labor force, Patrick started the crowdfunded Community Clothing label. The brand has been set up as a manufacturers' cooperative, offering "seasonless" garment essentials - such as socks and shirts - made during those dreaded production lulls. By no means a panacea, it's a social experiment stitched into a sound enough business model that may make a real difference. As in Patrick's other ventures, the priorities include accessibility in pricing, low waste, and high quality. Excised from the equation are marketing expenditures and inventory surplus to stay on-point with sustaining the jobs.

Patrick continues to support small, independent businesses as well, sourcing materials from the likes of Hebridean weaver Donald John Mackay of Luskentyre, the family-owned Breanish Tweed, and John R. MacLean of Garynahine. And he is also optimistic about the market's competence in recognizing better made garments. "The way men dress in London, as well as New York, is changing in ways that encourage them to have fun again," he notes. "In our ready to wear collections, we do play with colors and prints. And in cutting, we try to come up with an interesting shape but we'll do it in a classic fabric. Or we'll take something like a classic Chesterfield and we'll use a daring bold check to encourage men to be more audacious with their clothes while keeping them ageless. It's important for us to make clothes that function and last. And tweed fulfills that in many ways."

- - - - - - - -

Outside of the fashion industry, few may be aware that the late Lee Alexander McQueen (1969-2010) got his start on Savile Row. This didn't make it any less a homecoming when, in 2013, the brand bearing his name opened a ready-to-wear and bespoke menswear shop at No. 9 Savile Row (while the flagship women's wear store is at Old Bond Street).

Still in his teens in the mid 1980s, McQueen applied for apprenticeship at Alexander & Sheppard (Est. 1906 and today housed at 32 Old Burlington Street) where he is believed to have mastered sewing a forward fitting in just two years (as opposed to an average of three). His training continued on briefly as pattern cutter at Gieves & Hawkes (Est. 1771, at No 1 Savile Row) before he fully explored his potential in women's wear via working at Romeo Gigli and studying at Central Saint Martins, the highly regarded arts and design college. From his 1992 "Jack the Ripper Stalks His Victims" graduation collection onward, McQueen has been praised for using his impressive skills in traditional craft and ruthlessly slashing garments to create things so breathtakingly new.

To those who had met McQueen, his shyness was obvious. No matter how high his star ascended or how deafening the cheers, it's a fair conjecture the unease he felt in his own skin never quite dissipated. He was prone to fits of belligerence, transparent defensiveness and the outward expression of his feelings of being misunderstood. Addictions borne out in public were also symptomatic of this. But even his most strident detractors couldn't deny his genius or his demiurgeous creations, supported as they always were by a deep understanding of the intrinsic properties of fabric and how they convey shape as well as history and culture. Because he rarely resorted to woven textiles, it was all the more wondrous whenever they appeared in a collection.

Often honoring his Scottish heritage in his work, McQueen chose the Autumn/Winter 2006-2007 Collection to use a tweed suit for the opening. Dubbed "The Widows of Culloden" in reference to the women who lost their husbands in the Battle of Culloden, this was viewed by most fashion editors as a less incendiary and more poetic return to some of the themes McQueen used in his 1995 "Highland Rape" Collection. Set against a soundtrack mix of bagpipes, howling winds, and mournful music from various film scores, the showing featured romanticized tartan dresses (particularly those using the black, red, and yellow McQueen sett) with traditional Scottish style draping over one shoulder and around the neck, tartan crinolines, and antique brocades.

A sophisticated nod to gamekeeping tradition, the tweed ensembles were crowned by grouse and mallard-feathered fascinators by acclaimed milliner Philip Treacy. The single-breasted tweed suit that opened the show was in brown with fur lapels and was worn with a fascinator, upon which a nest containing seven blue eggs embellished by Swarovski crystals was artfully perched. It was crafted by brilliant jewelry designer Shaun Leane, who was among Lee's closest friends and trusted collaborators. He says, "How Lee and I worked together would vary each season. Sometimes he would show me the mood board, explain the collection and concept, and I would proceed to come up with ideas and designs. On this occasion, he wanted couture jewelry, made from valuable materials and gemstones (rendered with) elements of fine setting and detailed craftsmanship harking back to my traditional training." In this sense, it was an unexpected and thrilling departure from Shaun's previous sculptural creations for McQueen such as the coil metal corset in "The Overlook" Autumn/Winter 1999 collection and the Tahitian pearl collar in "What a Merry Go-Round" Autumn/Winter 2001 collection.

In coming up with this piece to accent the tweed suit, Shaun recalls, "I suggested pavé set jeweled eggs in a nest hand woven with sterling silver twigs. The eggs were set with over 800 blue topaz and smoky quartz stones. Once I started to craft the elements together, I met with Phillip to discuss how we could fuse our disciplines in constructing the piece." This then led to the creation of a bookend piece that appeared later in the same show. Whereas the nest headdress was meant to symbolize birth, the companion Eagle skull piece says Shaun was "to celebrate death, thus leaving the door open to rebirth. Completely pavé set with over a thousand brown topaz stones and eye sockets with black spinels. The skull was of blacked sterling silver, and decorated with a black feather bloom arranged by Phillip."

Shaun's memories of Lee carry with them not just the satisfaction of having collaborated on masterworks but also genuine and deep affection. He says, "Those were very exciting, freeing and creative times. I loved working with Lee because he pushed all boundaries. We would energize each other with possibilities." For Shaun, the creation of the tweed suit in collaboration with the millinery and jewelry effectively evoked "the feeling of the Highlands of Scotland". In 2017, Shaun was persuaded to relinquish some of his esoteric collaborations with Lee, which were placed on the auction block by Sothebys. The Skeleton Corset ("Untitled" Spring/Summer 1999 Collection), last seen in Madonna's 2004 Re-Invention Tour video and photography shoots by Steven Klein and Craig McDean, doubled its high estimate at the drop of the hammer with the collection fetching a higher than projected $2.6 M in total sales.

After McQueen's tragic passing, Sarah Burton, who had by then been with the house for over a decade, assumed the mantle of creative director. She started as a 21 year-old intern and went on to absorb the designer's creative methods even as she was being encouraged to find her own technique. She had the unenviable task of completing McQueen's unfinished "Angels & Demons" Autumn/Winter 2010 Collection. It was a medieval meditation on saints and sinners that the fashion press sanctified as "pure McQueen". Burton would achieve another personal triumph when she created the bridal gown for Catherine (née Middleton), the now Duchess of Cambridge, for her wedding to Prince William, Duke of Cambridge. Burton has thereafter proven herself more than qualified to steer the label with a sense of continuity while imprinting on it her own sensibilities.

Since she took over, Burton has fostered style for the empowered woman to a greater degree than her predecessor. While her signature has attained distinction, a line may still be drawn directly from McQueen to Burton's sincere appreciation for craft and the decision to open the Savile Row shop. She worked closely with David Collins (1955-2013), the late Irish architect and interior designer in refurbishing No. 9 Savile Row as the McQueen menswear outpost. The shop's light and modern feel is contrasted by McQueen's beloved Victorian and gothic flourishes, evident in the claw-foot display cases and the spine-like clothes railings. And yes, there are tweeds aplenty. In keeping with tradition, the in-house bespoke tailoring service is below stairs. Here, they specialize in McQueen's signature 'pagoda shoulder' jackets with suits typically cut closer to the body that count A-list celebrities like Tom Hiddleston and Benedict Cumberbatch as fans.

— — — — — — — —

Unfortunately, possessing the most unimpeachable of pedigrees won't guarantee survival. History is littered by the ruins of houses brought down by the vagaries of fashion, the skyrocketing costs of commercial rents, and the quotidian worries of maintaining a viable business. Hardie Amies at No. 8 Savile Row (with its official headquarters at No. 14) had reportedly been operating on substantial losses for a while that it was forced into entering administration. Failing to secure a buyer, it finally had to shutter in January 2019. Once before in 2008, the brand had faced imminent closure when it was rescued by a subsidiary of private equity firm Fung Capital. This time, despite vigorous campaigns to reboot the label for modern shoppers with an expanded ready-to-wear line, no white knight stepped up to save the day. One posited theory is that after the late Sir Edwin Hardy Amies' (1909-2003) retirement, the absence of a formidable enough principal (such as Norton & Son's Patrick Grant or Karl Lagerfeld at Chanel) made the brand's decline an inevitability. The equation of the house to its namesake was too strong and finding someone to follow Sir Edwin was always going to be difficult even in the most ideal of circumstances.

Once dressmaker-by-appointment (from 1955 to 1989) to HM Queen Elizabeth II, Sir Edwin was largely known for his work in women's wear. He began his career as couturier at Lachasse in 1933. London was already peerless in men's tailoring and its women's wear was beginning to receive similar notice. Sir Edwin's prominence rose in 1937 after he came out with a suit he called "Panic", made of Linton tweed in sage green with cerise overcheck, and it was photographed for American Vogue by Cecil Beaton. One of Sir Edwin's most consequential contributions to women's fashion was to render a more pleasing silhouette by cutting not along the natural waistline but just above the hip. He introduced his eponymous women's wear label in 1945 and tellingly at No. 14 Savile Row, which he found as little more than a war-torn shell of a property before giving it a complete restoration.

His first foray into menswear in 1959 was with a ready-to-wear line in collaboration with Joseph Hepworth & Son (Est. 1864, now called Next). It is believed that Sir Edwin's frustration with his female clients' conservative requirements led him to indulge his bolder ideas on menswear not just through design but with then fresh though now standard practices. In 1961, Hardy Amies held one of the earliest menswear runway shows at the Lancaster Ballroom of the Savoy Hotel with the present-day archetypal format of being musically scored and closing with the appearance of the designer taking a bow with the models. A few years later, Sir Edwin released his quippy manual "ABC of Men's Fashion" and followed that up by creating costumes for the Stanley Kubrick 1968 sci-fi classic "2001: A Space Odyssey". Coincidentally, a scene from the motion picture was shot in the Outer Hebrides. Ironically, the very future of the house is now uncertain.

V

Dark Clouds Bursting in a Perfect Sky

Garment manufacturing in New York City has been circling the drain for a while now. It's a distressing matter, particularly for those who depend on these middle income jobs, as well as to those who know that the rag trade was the largest manufacturing sector of the city for the past several generations. According to reports culled from the New York State Department of Labor and the US Census Bureau, the industry's workforce has receded at alarming rates, exacerbated by a nationwide trend of migrating production offshore. In covering the story of the contentious rezoning of New York's fabled garment district (the area encompassing Broadway to Ninth Avenue, from W35th to W40th streets), the Associated Press placed the estimate at only 5,000 workers left in 2018. And the problem is not confined to New York. Worldwide, other cities and regions that once thrived on high quality garment manufacturing, even for large scale production, have all similarly lost these jobs to China, India, Bangladesh, and Vietnam. Though appreciably unrelated for an argument of causation, a correlation is discernible in many instances between the dwindling of manufacturing and defaulting to tourism as a source of revenue. During an on-air commentary, former late night wag Jon Stewart once quipped, in a throw-away line, about New York's "parade-based economy". Jokes are funny when they're true. Or at least close enough to the truth to hurt. And that one was a knee-slapper.

Even on the relatively remote Isle of Lewis and Harris, tourists are now arriving with the regularity of those swallows at Capistrano. Fortunately for the locals, the onslaught of visitors hasn't been anywhere so frenzied as the stampede during rope drop at Disneyworld. And that day may never arrive. But the signs of alleged "progress" have docked on these shores anyway. Already there's a hipster-bait microbrewery on the island. And by the piers on Tarbert there recently opened a distillery marketing gin infused with botanicals and a single malt scheduled to launch in 2020. But it's the businesses that grind on production methods now deemed irrefutably archaic and therefore cost prohibitive that are particularly vulnerable.

The specificity of how Harris Tweed is crafted is practically hewn in stone; and purists are wont to take umbrage at the slightest deviation. For instance, when it became apparent that the industry at large began requiring double-width cloth instead of the 29-inch wide standard woven on Hattersley looms, a proposal to amend the statutes governing the certification of genuine Harris Tweed in favor of sanctioning the change was still voted down. Although originally put in place to guarantee standards and authenticity, these same methods have paradoxically prevented it from rivaling synthetic fabrics and hampered its ability to keep up with quixotic fashion trends. Then again, doing so has never really been the agenda. And whether it is or isn't crucial now continues to be controversial. Still, there's no disputing the figures. In the 1960s, some two thousand Hebrideans pedaled away on treadle-powered looms to produce over seven million yards of Harris Tweed annually. But the succeeding decades witnessed a waning of interest and a steady decline in orders.

The American and Japanese markets that had once been so dependable had gradually switched allegiances to other sources. Evidence of attrition became all too glaring when the big mills at Stornoway shuttered and the number of still employed mill workers plummeted to 100 while only 150 at-home weavers were left. On the whole, annual production of Harris Tweed was down to only 700,000 yards by the 2000s. And it seemed like nothing could stem the bleeding. But as hopes dimmed into abysmal despair, along came a Yorkshire-based businessman called Brian Haggas who swooped in to buy the Kenneth Mackenzie Mill. The mill had been on the selling block for four years and accounted for much of the meager volume of Harris Tweed production. Haggas, of the textile firm The John Haggas Group, had also completed purchase of another tweed mill at Parkend on the Isle of Lewis, as well as the clothing manufacturer Brook Taverner Ltd. To the islanders, a turnaround appeared within reach. Or so it seemed.

So providential had been Haggas' arrival, there was little reason to look the gift businessman in the mouth. And given the dire situation, few were willing. Thus suppressing whatever instinctive mistrust the locals harbored for all outsiders, they welcomed Haggas with open arms. He sauntered into Kenneth Mackenzie brimming with ideas. It's a pity they weren't particularly sensible ones. First, he deemed it a costly prospect to continue producing an enormous inventory of colors and patterns. He decided from then on that the mill was going to churn out only four, which Patrick at Norton & Sons described as "brown, brown, slightly blue, grey and brown". Second, Haggas decided that these patterns would now only be used for making one style jacket, which he intended to sell exclusively. Because, sure, why not?

The islanders were almost unanimously aghast. Any goodwill Haggas had received when first he came, along with whatever hope it had briefly flickered, was quickly extinguished. To the press, Haggas explained his strategy as streamlining, arguing that not only was this move more commercially sound, but having a singular Harris Tweed jacket in the market would no doubt restore the cloth's luster. Industry observers were understandably skeptical, pointing out that this bold move meant Haggas was effectively isolating the supply of Harris Tweed. With a cornered market he would be artificially creating scarcity. And weren't there still wholesale customers, however few, to take into account? The island's local weavers decided to hold a meeting, which resulted in more heated squabbling over what recourses to take. Options that were considered included going on strike or competing with Haggas directly by buying another mill. But a work moratorium would've been like cutting off the nose to spite the face. And the weavers knew that, even with their combined resources, raising enough capital to put another mill into operation was too far-fetched. It's a good thing pitchforks and torches were left off the table.

In 2006, chatter around the island crescendoed when someone from Ralph Lauren was rumored to have arrived. Speculation ran rampant as said individual had been observed inquiring about the possibility of either leasing or purchasing outright the Shawbost Mill, which had been in abeyance for two years. Yet again, however, hopes were dashed when any discussions that may have begun went nowhere. Instead, a collective sigh of relief did transpire a year later when Shawbost was at last acquired. Ian Angus Mackenzie, a former chief executive of the Harris Tweed Authority; Ian Taylor, global CEO of independent energy trader The Vitol Group; and Brian Wilson, the former UK Labour Minister got together to set up Harris Tweed Hebrides at Shawbost to pick up production.

- - - - - - - -

Several people with small businesses reliant on the supply of Harris Tweed ended up turning to Harris Tweed Hebrides. Among them was designer Catherine Aitken. She handcrafts stylish accessories including messenger bags, rucksacks, and stoles from her Leith studio in Edinburgh. Upon hearing ambivalent accounts of the Kenneth Mackenzie mill situation, she decided to find out what was going on for herself and traveled to Lewis and Harris. When she got there, she was relieved to learn that because the volume of her order was relatively paltry she was still able to procure supplies for her line. But she says, "Aside from Harris Tweed Hebrides, I source from small individual suppliers anyway because they don't require minimum size orders and are happy to make me a short run of a particular color or pattern. I think if mine was a larger business, the situation at the mills would have been inescapably problematic."

And so Catherine realized she was alright, for the moment. Unfortunately, any form of certainty moving forward was not forthcoming. "It was definitely a worry for the future," she concluded, returning to Edinburgh with her supplies. But as many others in her position, worry she did. Her label is based on the use of heritage cloth and while she could have potentially resorted to her other mainstays - Fife linens and waxed cottons from Dundee - losing Harris Tweed would've dealt a serious blow to her livelihood.

Catherine muses about her earliest memories of tweed, "I grew up in a household of traditional Scottish garments, grandmothers in mohair capes, father and grandfather in Harris Tweed jackets and kilts. An uncle of mine was a kilt-maker. And one of my grandmothers made us clothes out of tweed and tartan." She laughingly recalls, "The first tweed garment I ever had was a kilt jacket, second hand from my cousin. I was probably about 7 or 8. At that age, I doubt I noticed how the jacket and kilt was such a boyish ensemble because my sisters and I all ended up wearing them. As you can imagine we were not the most fashion forward youngsters back then!" And so fashion wasn't her first choice as a career either. She started instead as a film and television producer of documentaries and a script consultant for BBC Scotland Drama. One year, she was attending the Cannes Film Festival to try and get financing for a film project. On an inspired whim, she designed some printed fabric handbags and brought them along as promotional items. She had hoped to make a favorable impression with them but was caught entirely off guard by the enthusiastic response they engendered at the festival. "People liked the bags so much, I thought then perhaps I could make some more, maybe start a small business."

Having had no previous experience in this field, Catherine wisely elected to go with what she already knew - those fabrics native to Scotland, sewing (which she learned from her grandmother), and bags. She says, "I have always loved bags, especially those in old movies starring Doris Day and Bette Davis, or in any Hitchcock film. Lauren Bacall has the cutest little Dorothy bag in 'To Have and Have Not'. Today, film buffs will notice that some of the mainstays in my collection are homages to old movie stars like the 'Hepburn Backpack' inspired by Katharine Hepburn's androgynous style. My 'Hayworth' handbag is a reflection of Rita Hayworth's shape." Catherine also has a clutch, the Voyager, which she conceived as a tribute to Irving Rapper's (1898-1999) "Now Voyager" from 1942. In that motion picture, Bette Davis (1908-1989) undergoes a Cinderella-like metamorphosis from a timid insecure woman to a radiant beauty, aided by stunning Orry-Kelly (1897-1964) dresses, veiled hats, and a succession of clutches.

In the beginning, designing the collection was done in Catherine's spare time. She carried on with her film and television production work while she was still trying to figure out how to get a fashion business off the ground. She met a fashion journalist who imparted helpful guidance on how to produce a cohesive collection and how to develop a website for e-commerce. It wouldn't be long before her day job lost her interest. And henceforth Catherine concentrated solely on her fashion brand. By the second collection, for which she created an array of bags entirely from upcycled vintage Harris Tweed jackets and kilts, the key elements of her line had come into perfect focus. She may derive artistic cues from the past but her designs have always been unmistakably contemporary and functionally relevant. And around the world, her customers agree. She says, "Scandinavia and the US have been consistently strong markets for my brand and I make special collections for high end retailers now like the British Museum and Victoria & Albert."

The current collection features bestselling messenger bags and backpacks, sized to carry laptops, some with extended flaps that can fold over or be used to increase capacity. Heritage and modern are cogently juxtaposed in the bristly tweed and smooth Scottish deerskin leather, in the use of pliant fabric as geometric frames, and in the Mondrian-like patchwork of different tweeds on the "Explorer" bag. That Catherine's pieces don't come down an assembly line in the thousands lend more cachet. And she is perfectly content to keep the business on this cottage industry scale, "In Scotland there's a lot of mass produced tweed and tartan accessories. I like to think I offer something that reflects the beauty and origin of tweeds, handmade with care and skill in Edinburgh by myself and a small group of artisans." That sentiment, along with her repurposing of old tweeds, has also earned her the admiration of environmental groups. The publicly-funded, non-profit organization Zero Waste Scotland has commissioned collections from her for its campaigns to affect ecological responsibility in policy, businesses, and individuals.

Additionally, Catherine has become an emissary for tweed and Scotland, having been asked by the government on several occasions to create Harris Tweed accessories as gifts to visiting dignitaries. For the 2007 Cinema China Film Festival in Edinburgh, she created an original handbag for the lauded Chinese actress Maggie Cheung (who was already enshrined in the fashion pantheon for wafting up and down stairs and along noirishly-lit corridors wearing the most ravishing *qípáos* in director Wong Kar Wai's 2001 masterpiece "In the Mood for Love",). Catherine has also represented her country at various events in the US including the "Dress to Kilt" runway show in New York. She says, "I have a real emotional connection to tweed because of my family, I feel very at home working with it and I think people will always find something new to discover in tweed."

- - - - - - - - -

Over a three-month period that began in late 2007, Haggas proceeded with his plan. There is enough room to debate the rectitude of Haggas' intentions. As a businessman, he can hardly be faulted for coming up with an "on paper" surefire profit-driven strategy. After taking over, his Kenneth Mackenzie mill made close to a hundred fifty thousand yards of tweed. Of course, the much needed work wasn't any less appreciated by the locals, but there was no quelling the communal foreboding. Haggas sent the tweeds to manufacturers in China where they were made into countless copies of the same style jacket. The finished pieces were then shipped back and packaged in elegant hunter green boxes with mahogany coat hangers as "genuine UK-certified" Harris Tweed products. Thus, with a Yorkshire warehouse full of Harris Tweed jackets in every size, all ready to be sold to retailers, Haggas waited for the money to roll in. To the surprise of no one but Haggas, the orders never came.

In the aftermath of the debacle, production ground to an almost immediate and total halt. Soon enough the first round of layoffs commenced as Haggas tried in vain to sell his merchandise. Even following a price reduction from around $400 a jacket to a steeply discounted $90, there was still a dearth of takers. In 2009, the few workers left on the payroll clocked out of Kenneth Mackenzie for the last time, leaving behind a mill cluttered by bolts of tweed with nowhere to go. The locals now felt worse off than before Haggas first showed up. Many could only wearily shake their heads, having thought this a doomed prospect all along. Wasn't Haggas just the latest in a line of outsiders who've come here unbidden, primed with grandiose if sometimes harebrained schemes that were supposed to better the lives of the island's inhabitants? Hadn't William Lever (1851-1925), the 1st Viscount Leverhulme, tried and failed miserably with his outlandish plans?

Lever, or Lord Leverhulme as he was called, once owned the Isle of Lewis and Harris. He arrived in the early 1900s, took residence at Lews Castle in Stornoway, and promptly announced his desire to improve the lives of everyone by tapping all of the island's natural resources to build a fishing empire, develop farms, set up chemical and power plants, and create a sprawling railway system. There's no denying that Lord Leverhulme's goals were benevolent. But his was the kind of philanthropy that could only be executed on his terms or not at all. Problems materialized at every conceivable juncture as Lord Leverhulme tried to wrest cooperation from the natives. The main point of contention had to do with how the land was to be used. And for all his intransigence, and the years and vast financial resources spent trying to realize his ambition, the hurdles proved truly insurmountable. Lord Leverhulme's plans ultimately collapsed under the weight of fanciful goals and local resistance. He conceded defeat in 1923. Yes, that was close to a hundred years ago, but memories have a way of lingering on this island. There can be no doubt Lord Leverhulme's name was murmured often and by many with respect to the Haggas situation.

As for Haggas, what seemed starkly obvious to everyone in the Outer Hebrides (and beyond) was that he had committed a business mistake so obvert it's a wonder it still happens with such ubiquity. He failed to understand his own product. It doesn't require 20/20 hindsight to see that by eliminating the astonishing varieties and colors of tweed, he effectively excised the most intrinsic part of what makes it exceptional in the first place. Defiant, Haggas positioned himself as the aggrieved party who simply sought to revive the failing industry. He pointed the finger of blame predictably at everything and everyone else, from the fabric itself to the apparently recalcitrant consumers. In various statements issued to the media, Haggas mounted his exculpatory defense squarely on the claim of having guilelessly assumed there was a clamoring for tweed only to regretfully discover that there wasn't. What he left out entirely was that it was what he was selling that did not exactly induce clamoring. In fairness to Haggas however, had his rather dubious plan actually worked he'd have been hailed as a hero. Regardless, the ruckus did generate spirited conversations about tweed not just in Scotland but across the pond. And new players with more to say were about to enter the fray.

- - - - - - - -

Surely the prospect of pouring money into the Harris Tweed industry as it was deteriorating in the early aughts must have given anyone serious pause. And viewed from the distance of a New York businessman's armchair, it must have been as welcoming as the sight of frantically waving red semaphore flags. So it's all the more baffling that American Scottish businessman Alan Lind Bain would not only go on to invest his own hard-earned dollars but more work into another failing Harris Tweed mill - Carloway. And yet, to those who knew him, this would make all the sense in the world.

Alan represents a curious trichotomy. He was born and raised a Londoner. He somehow possesses, to this day, an innately New York work ethic. Yet in his soul, he can only be characterized as a true son of Scotland. Anyone who knows Alan will attest that he has a heart as wide and open as the skies of his ancestral home. The only child of Scottish parents, he grew up at the onset of the second world war. He says, "My Dad was Aberdonian by birth and spent his working life in the jute industry as a sales manager based in London where he met my mother. They both took great pride in their heritage. My mother earned an OBE for her lifelong dedication to community service. And they exemplified those post WWII principles of service to family, community, and country." Because he was being reared in London, his family took extra care in ensuring he would not fully lose touch with his Scottish lineage. When he was around six, he recalls being outfitted with his very first kilt. But to his mortification, as he was walking down the street, he overheard someone commenting on his "nice looking skirt".

There were also scores of aunts, uncles, and cousins who drifted in and out of his life to further stress their shared roots. After the war ended and petrol was no longer in short supply, the family traveled every year on holidays. They often took meandering road trips to Scotland and followed routes that enabled them to visit and stay with relatives. "My mother's sister Mae usually hosted us on those excursions. She initiated me into the delights of many traditional dishes like fried duck eggs with bacon. We would have breakfasts of black and white pudding, herring kippers, and oatmeal porridge; while lunch or dinner would mean haggis or local salmon," he recounts. "I wasn't aware of it then but all those helped shape my appreciation for Scotland." He continues, "The family home is situated in Wormit, a small town at the end of the Tay Rail Bridge. The bridge was visible from the windows of my uncle's house and I still vividly remember the hours I would spend watching those steam trains that ran through it." Little did he know then that his journeys would take him much farther than anywhere those trains were headed.

When he attended Mill Hill School (Est 1807) he was asked to share his room with an American called Ned Bradley, who he tormented with an endless barrage of questions about the US. Alan recalls that after putting up with it for a while, Ned finally snapped at him, "If you're so interested, why don't you go there?!" Alan decided that he would do so. Ned, on the other hand, remembers the incident a little differently. Today, Ned is better known as Professor of Classics emeritus Edward M. Bradley at Dartmouth (Est 1769). "I was one of many American prep school boys (who were placed in schools in the UK) through an English-Speaking Union scholarship. According to Ned, "Alan was often an extravagant fellow, always of cheerful humor and high spirits. To be sure, he was curious about life in America. And I think that I must have encouraged him to consider applying for the same scholarship I had." Indeed Alan sent in an application and was granted one that allowed him to study as an exchange student in the US, at the Connecticut prep school founded by and named after Frederick W. Gunn known as The Gunnery (Est 1850).

It was at The Gunnery that Alan made the acquaintance of his first wife Linda née Miller (1937-2006), who was attending the nearby St Margaret's School in Waterbury, CT. It was a fairly easygoing courtship and they were married in 1957. As a wedding present, one of Alan's uncles gifted them with a full length of their clan's Mackay tweed. Alan says, "We loved that tweed." Part of it was used to upholster a chair Alan uses to this day. Shortly after though, they had to move to the UK so Alan could complete his degree in jurisprudence at Cambridge. While living there, they welcomed their firstborn, a daughter they named Heather. They also eventually had a son they called Ian. After being admitted to the bar by the Honourable Society of the Inner Temple, Alan decided that instead of becoming a British solicitor, he was far more interested in practicing international law.

The family returned to the US where they settled in New York while Alan went to Columbia University (Est 1754). He graduated in 1964 with an LLB law degree, all set for a long career. Or so he thought. He had already taken to the city like a puddle duck to the Hudson River. But New York also ignited that restless energy he's always had. It would henceforth fuel a persistent impulse to achieve, thus setting him on a completely different path. It was in the course of dealing with international clients for his law practice that he struck on an idea. Despite the shortness of their stays, these men still needed to conduct business, often from their hotel rooms. Alan thought why couldn't he provide them (along with other traveling businessmen) with temporary use office spaces, conference rooms, and support staff? After putting together some capital, Alan opened World-Wide Business Centres on Madison Avenue in 1970, still there to this day, and a forerunner to the now booming field of shared work spaces. It was then that Alan formally joined the ranks of New York's entrepreneurial citizenry.

But the more attached he grew to New York the more Alan felt the incessant pull of his homeland. In order to renew his bond to Scotland, in 1986 he signed up to join the local American-Scottish Foundation (ASF). Conceived in 1956 by Lord Malcolm Avondale Douglas-Hamilton (1909-1964), the foundation fortifies ties between Americans of Scottish descent and Scottish expats and their home country through charitable, cultural, and social projects. It was during Lord Malcolm's second marriage to the American Natalie Scarritt (1909-2013) née Wales of Cohasset, Massachusetts that he came to view the US as his adopted country and thereafter became actively involved in Scottish American causes.

Though they had never met, Alan shared much of Lord Malcolm's zeal for the foundation's goals. His earnest and enthusiastic participation assured his appointment as president of the ASF in 1993. At first, he did waver over the immensity of the position's scope and what that may entail. "I accepted only on a three-year trial basis," he says. "But shortly after, the potential of a Scottish parliament became a reality. I realized the ASF had a role to play in the things happening back there and that I needed to accept this important responsibility." Early into his days in office, he led the formation of the Scottish Coalition that brought together various organizations in pushing for the celebration of a National Tartan Day on April 6. The date is a commemoration of the original Declaration of Arbroath letter sent to Pope John XXII in

1320 asserting Scotland's rights as a kingdom independent from the rule of England's Norman monarchy. On having an official Tartan Day Alan says, "We wanted to find a way of bringing together Scottish Americans as a united and proud group. And tartan is a powerful symbol we could all rally behind." With help from Senator Chester Trent Lott Sr., the American celebration of National Tartan Day received ratification from the US Senate in 1998. Alan recalls how they held their first parade in New York. "We didn't have the sense back then to file for a permit. We had no idea how to hold a parade so we just got together and walked the street," he laughs.

Another one of Alan's duties as foundation president found him overseeing a charity gathering for the Highland Fund (Est. 1953), which incidentally was also founded by Lord Malcolm. Representing the Highland Fund during the fundraiser was a classmate of Alan's from Cambridge called Cameron Bannerman. Alan asked his old friend where the $15,000 raised that evening was being earmarked. Bannerman replied that the donation was going toward purchasing a prototype double-width loom for the Harris Tweed industry to promote more efficient cutting and less wastage of cloth. Alan found this interesting but otherwise thought little more of it until a few years later when he and Linda were on holiday in Scotland. They spontaneously decided to take a detour to the Outer Hebrides and see for themselves how the ASF donation had been spent and how the tweed industry was faring. The sorry state of affairs they found there galvanized Alan into taking action.

Alan's daughter Heather (who served as director of the ASF and currently still serves as chairman emerita), recalls that fateful decision and says it was one her father couldn't resist. She says, "My father has always held a deep sense of longing for Scotland. But I believe that after we lost my grandfather, he must've felt an even stronger sense of family responsibility to keep that connection to the old world." Heather says family tradition was always important to the Bains. When her paternal grandmother was still alive, Grandma B (for Bain), as she was called, was ensconced at Blackberry Hill Farm, a rambling 300 acre farmstead in New Hampshire where the entire family got together for Christmas and summer vacations. There, Grandma B would host her own version of Highland Games in which they all had to participate. Heather also recalls how Grandma B endeared herself to the local butchers who were initially confused by her requests to buy lamb offal, which she used to make her own haggis.

Heather says her father's work at the ASF was an important way of staying in touch with other Scots in the US. But the agendas of its many chapters became increasingly more compartmentalized while Alan was set on a unified and direct involvement to Scotland itself. Plus, she asserts, "My father approaches business as a problem solver and the whole tweed situation in the Outer Hebrides played into that along with his love for Scotland. It troubled my Dad that the tweed industry, such a critical aspect of Scottish culture, was in peril. And there seemed to be little being done about it. Somehow he decided that he could and therefore had to help turn the tide."

Alan says, "Seeing the situation first hand was deeply frustrating to me. Other countries invest in the protection and preservation of their national treasures. And Harris Tweed is an endangered part of Scottish culture. Why wasn't more being done? Why was there no government support?" He also lamented over what he perceived as a somewhat fatalistic attitude among the locals toward a problem that could be fixed. He resolved to do something about it himself. In 2005 Alan met Dr. Sheila Brock, who was fundraising for the Museum of Scotland. He confided in her his thoughts on the matter. It was at her recommendation that he then went to see Derek Reid (1944-2019) who had acquired Carloway mill two years prior. According to Heather, "My dad and Derek got along like a house on fire." Although *fait* was pretty much *accompli* by then. One way or another, Alan was going to help. He invested his own money with Reid into improving Harris Tweed Textiles Ltd.'s Carloway mill. It had been in desperate financial straits for a while and Alan had shown up at an opportune moment. He also took on an active role in the company, serving as its North American agent, while Reid continued the day-to-day running of the place. And like Haggas at

Kenneth McKenzie, Alan had ideas on how to rebuild the industry. The crucial difference was Alan was as vested in the pastoral roots of Harris Tweed as he was in seeking ways to secure its future.

For many years, Alan traveled to Scotland twice annually to help with work at the mill. He also enlisted the aid of Martin Hunt, who today still heads Edinburgh and Inverness-based public relations agency Tartan Silk. Alan was sure tweed and the industry itself could use some good old-fashioned hype. He and Hunt were of the same mind that the way forward in reversing Harris Tweed's depreciated reputation was to re-invigorate its prestige bona fides without abandoning its core qualities. Alan recognized advantageous points that might resonate with the modern shopper. "There's renewed interest in the luxury arena for sustainability and artisanal products. I believe tweed would align well in high style and appeal to the young."

- - - - - - - -

Before he got into PR, Martin Hunt was already trumpeting the best of Scotland through his previous work at Bingham, Hughes and Macpherson, Chartered Surveyors. Throughout the 1970s, his job took him on trips all across the Highlands and the Western Isles and aroused his affection for the land. In 1982, he moved to Edinburgh to work for estate agents Bell Ingram where he took on the duties of press secretary. It was such a fulfilling experience that he was motivated to go into public relations, moving briefly to London in order to shore up requisite media contacts. When he returned to Scotland in 1990, Martin worked deliberately with industries that had environmental portfolios. Seven years later, he opened Tartan Silk. Alan and Martin met through Alice Wood, a work colleague of Martin's. "Alan and I immediately struck up an excellent friendship. In 2006, he asked me to help raise the profile of Carloway." Martin accepted without hesitation. He had built his PR agency for exactly these projects. "We promote all that is praiseworthy about Scotland," he says, "and I grew up wearing the kilt and Harris

Tweed jackets as part of our school uniform. What could be more Scottish than Harris Tweed?"

In direct opposition to Haggas' ploy, Martin trotted out Carloway's tweeds to a wider audience and endorsed the richness of its diversity in patterns, contemporary colors, and collateral applications. In 2007, he staged a tweeded-up Victorian armchair as the centerpiece window display at Brooks Brothers in London. Drawing more media attention was the joint effort he arranged between Carloway and the Edinburgh-based and family-owned Eastern Western Motor Group (Est. 1927). Together, they had the car seats and interior door panels of an Alfa Romeo MiTo upholstered in a specially-designed black and (Alfa Romeo) red stripes and offered it as a custom option to buyers. A fashion model, dressed in a captivating Harris Tweed cape coat designed by Isabel Wong, posed alongside the sportscar during the launch. Martin revisited this concept, curiously enough, to celebrate the centenary of another publicity stunt. To commemorate the anniversary of when Henry Alexander Jr, (the son of Scotland's first Ford dealer) drove a Model T up to the summit of Britain's highest mountain, Ben Nevis, Caroloway upholstered the interiors of a Model T Ford that was displayed at a vintage car rally.

Of course, it wasn't all newsworthy staged photo ops. Martin assisted Alan with several visits from important fabric buyers by finessing the brand message of Harris Tweed for the foreign market. Martin recalls though that being non-islanders, his and Alan's efforts were often met with "a degree of resistance" by the locals. They carried on undeterred, at least for a while. Regrettably, Martin's work began to outpace the PR budget. Even long after the account had accrued outstanding balances, Martin marshaled on out of his abiding friendship and respect for Alan. Today, Martin's Tartan Silk projects still involve worthy causes and a sense of heritage. He looks back on his work with Harris Tweed as having been driven by what Martin describes as "my passion to support Carloway and Alan in what he was endeavoring to achieve."

- - - - - - - -

Of import to Alan's long-term strategy to make Carloway competitive in the international market was the development of lighter versions of Harris Tweed, at par with the materials Linton Tweeds supplied to the fashion houses. Coincidentally, while Alan was getting Carloway to produce them, his assistant at the ASF in New York, Lusmila McColl had just been encouraged to participate as a designer in a charity event in Glasgow. Lusmila, whose mother hailed from Dumbarton, took her position at the ASF after completing some contract film work. On the lookout for a new gig, she had heard that the ASF needed help organizing Tartan Week and festivities for the organization's 50th anniversary. She landed the job and was still Alan's assistant when the opportunity to design for the charity show presented itself.

Although she never had formal training, Lusmila had spent most of her life dabbling in fashion. Her Brazilian Amazon father had taught her how to sew. She says, "Growing up, I felt I had an awkward body shape so I created my own clothes. It came out of necessity and enjoyment." The people who knew that the clothes she wore were of her own making pushed her to pursue fashion. Unfortunately, she says, "I never had the money to be able to afford to go to school for it, much less start a career." When the chance came to participate in the charity fashion show, she broached the topic to Alan, who was only too willing to help her create a collection using tweed as her main medium.

Lusmila admits she knew very little about tweed before she began working with the fabric. She laughs, "All I thought was that it was this heavy, cumbersome fabric rich white men wore to go hunting." She was dumbfounded to learn otherwise when she first saw what Carloway had to offer. She purposely asked Alan to provide her with discarded materials because she liked the idea of repurposing them into use for beautiful garments. "The mill had tons lying about," she recalls. "I immediately went for the lightweight tweeds drenched in purples, pinks, light blues, bright plaids - but I also used some traditional ones like grey herringbone." From the outset, she let the materials dictate to her how they wanted to take shape. She was also adamant about leaving raw edges and having less seaming in the finished garments to give emphasis to how they were crafted.

In November 2007, Carloway and Lusmila unveiled her capsule collection of eight pieces, made from single-width bolts of tweed, at the CatWalk charity fashion show in Glasgow to support the non-profit Maggie's Centre, which aids cancer patients and their families. The highlights included: a high-collar 'Dragon' coat, a green mini skirt kilt and top adorned by neon lace ribbon detail; a men's coat hybrid of Nehru and evening tails; and a smashing gown in black and grey herringbone tweed with contrasting fuchsia silk lining. The collection irrefutably validated Alan and Lusmila's confidence in Harris Tweed as a modern fabric. A biker jacket and trousers ensemble from the collection was worn by the rock singer Courtney Love later that year for a New Year's Eve performance in London.

There was however, a bittersweet note to the success of the showing. The fight to save the Harris Tweed industry was daunting for everyone involved. And from the outside, it appeared practically Sisyphean. Heather confides, "My father persevered at Carloway as long as he could for one other important reason." His wife, Heather's mother Linda, had been battling cancer and it was as if Alan's work at Carloway offered, if not necessarily a respite, at least a productive way of channeling his energies. Sadly, Linda did succumb to cancer in 2006. And it was for that reason that the CatWalk show benefiting cancer charity held such a poignant significance for Alan.

Another Carloway creation to make the news was a ravishing, white strapless wedding gown and coat for Gaelic singer Alyth McCormack who married Irish musician Noel Eccles in Aberdeenshire in 2009. The dress was created by the late Ann MacCallum (1962-2013) who designed under the label "Hebridean Dreams", and a year later, she became the first woman ever to manage a tweed mill, the Carloway. As for Lusmila, she continued to work with Alan for about two more years and once flew to Japan to represent the mill and Harris Tweed (and Scottish textiles in general) to the market there. But the financial pressures of a fashion business took their toll on Lusmila. She says, "Missing backing or support, managing your own fashion line is almost impossible. So, I had to let it go." Still, the experience has brought her back home. She relocated to Scotland in 2017 and got her citizenship. "It was something Heather (Bain) always encouraged me to do. So I finally did it and I couldn't be happier about it." Although she isn't in fashion anymore and is currently starting a wellness studio, she says, "I hope to get back into designing and finding ways I can contribute and promote this country I so love to the world."

Alan, meanwhile, was unable to sustain his long distance participation in Carloway Mill either. And with Reid practically running the company on his own, it wasn't long before it passed on to new owners Annie Macdonald and Anthony Loftus. After taking over in 2017, current management announced that all the mill workers were being retained with additional hires being planned as they hoped to build momentum from the introduction of the mill's lighter weight tweeds. From his home in New York, Alan keeps tabs on what's happening at the mill through many friends on the Outer Hebrides. Although weaving had resumed on the island, stability may be too optimistic a word for it. Turmoil and uncertainty have a way of circling back on the industry in Scotland. Still, Alan's faith in Harris Tweed has never faltered. He says, "Tweed is not something you discard after a season. It has been and will undoubtedly continue to be handed down from generation to generation."

VI

Ports in a Storm, Comfy and Cozy

The sheep's share, as it were, of credit for tweeds may often go to their neighbors to the North, but the Irish are just as proud of their own resplendent Donegal variety. Though they have been mostly impervious to the systemic vulnerabilities of the Scottish mills, manufacturers in Ireland still had to weather industry-wide fluctuations in demand. They did so by being more responsive to market shifts and exploring applications for the cloth traditionalists would rather overlook.

Like those from Scotland, tweeds made in Ireland were originally domestically hand spun and dyed. Donegals, however, were mostly identified by either their herringbone pattern or "salt and pepper" compositions, so-called for having tiny colorful knops ingrained in the material to give it sparkling effervescence. Today, there is none prouder of Donegals than Magee1866's Temple siblings who are directly descended from Robert Temple (1866-1958), cousin to founder John Magee (1849-1901). Temple joined the company as an apprentice at its drapers shop twenty years after Magee began dealing in woolen goods in the small towns of Ardara and Carrick in County Donegal, from whence the fabric gets its name.

The town of Ardara is historically noteworthy to tweed. It was a commercial hub for woolen goods, livestock, and produce when a market opened there in the late 1700s. By the next century, its craftspeople had organized themselves into making tweeds competitive enough to be sold farther afield. Overall improvements in quality came with the invention of the flying shuttle loom for increased production, the opening of a market house where the tweeds were carefully inspected, stored, and sold, and impressing upon the young an appreciation for the craft of weaving.

At Magee1866, in the meantime, Temple had made such valuable contributions in a few years that he was allowed to buy into the company in 1901. Nine years later, once Magee felt ready to retire, he let Temple buy him out completely. Under Temple's leadership, the company opened its own factory in 1918 and began to produce original patterns and designs. Although work was initially outsourced to a network of independent weavers, Temple also cultivated an in-house team at the factory for better quality control and to avoid the likelihood of patterns being copied. Business held steady through the years with Temple's son Howard eventually succeeding him, followed in the 1970s by Howard's son Lynn, who all but grew up at the factory and is still presently the company chairman.

When Lynn took over, everyone in the industry was going through the same downturn in demand. Unlike manufacturers in Scotland, however, Magee was able to avoid being swept by the undertow because it wasn't shackled to those statutes governing the making of Harris Tweed. The brand didn't have to sacrifice the time-honored craftsmanship of Donegal tweeds while it adopted cost-efficient power looms, and gradually moved along the currents of contemporary needs by producing business suits, and then more casual, "lifestyle"-driven designs, and a range of women's wear, which debuted in 1998.

That Lynn's own children joined the company in the 2000s has only helped in determining how to entice a new generation of shoppers. Son Patrick is CEO of Magee Weaving. Daughter Charlotte is design director. And daughter Rosy heads sales and marketing. Rosy says they were never pressured into becoming part of the company. Each of them actually pursued other careers first before, perhaps inevitably, coming home to Magee1866. She says this just shows how deeply this business runs in their blood. She is the first to agree the siblings and their father often have what she calls "robust conversations" about which directions to take. "We are very different people. And we are passionate about what we do. But at the end of the day, we are very much in agreement regarding what Magee1866 is about. Day-to-day differences of opinion don't matter so long as we appreciate the same key values. Besides, outside of work, we have many other shared interests like cycling or mackerel fishing that bond us closer."

She agrees it "sounds mad" for them to willingly get together on weekends after having spent the workweek in each other's companies, but it does make them appreciate each other more. And, they've all agreed on an iron-clad rule of restricting business talk to within the Magee1866 premises. At first, it was in deference to their mother, who didn't want her home turned into just another office space. But they soon realized that avoiding business discussions at home also helped company morale. "We all work together as a team with people who are as invested in the success of Magee1866 and have equally valid insights," she says. "It simply would not serve any purpose for the family to be off having private chats that no one is allowed to be part of then returning to the office and presenting everyone with irreversible decisions."

Those decisions are carefully weighed by Lynn and the children in service of forging ahead without violating what makes Magee1866 and Donegals salient. One such critical move by the company, given tweed's inherent qualities, is surveying new means of strengthening its sustainability protocols from closer source-to-shelf cycles and the utilization of green energy. When Rosy attended the 2019 Tokyo Tweed Run, she was genuinely moved by having learned of the Japanese word "*mottainai*". It has no corresponding term in the English language but may be described as "a sense of regret" over something that's been wasted and serves as an admonition for the long-term appreciation and use of anything in one's possession.

If tweed is to continue thriving in markets like Japan, Rosy at Magee1866 says paying heed to tradition while offering new fabrications is imperative. By way of an example, she points to how the same dedication goes toward the making of their fabrics for the classic group of Celtic tweeds as for the more experimental "fancy" varieties, which are used in two main categories. "At our weaving division, we create separate luxury fabrics from wool, linen, cashmere and silk made exclusively for international fashion labels and another range allocated for our own collections," she says. In 2015, the already extensive Magee1866 cloth inventory and archives were further augmented by its acquisition of the Robert Noble mill. This venerated company has been at its March Street location in Peebles, Scotland since 1884, but was already operating since 1666. With centuries of accumulated patterns, it's undoubtedly an invaluable addition to the Magee1866 portfolio. Rosy says, output from their Robert Noble mill of 100% lambswool, and blends of wool with cashmere or linen make beautiful lightweight fabrics for their warm weather jackets, suits, and coats.

When it comes to the designs, Rosy says her sister Charlotte works with two separate teams, one responsible for the fabrics and the other for the ready-to-wear collections. The cloth and the construction may speak on behalf of the brand's heritage but there is nary a trace of nostalgia in either the men's or women's ready-to-wear pieces. Here are sharply tailored garments that can and do stand side by side any other designer label at department stores across Ireland, the UK, and Europe. Apart from the brand's website, the collections are now also available at its South Anne Street flagship, which opened in 2016 to celebrate Magee1866's 150th year. The store, ensconced in a vibrant Dublin neighborhood, occupies two floors and showcases not just the garments but an accessories line (launched in 2012) of scarves, wallets, and belts, as well as an assortment of home-related goods from plush teddy bears, plaid throws, and coordinating pillows.

The company's foray into the shelter category is certainly a sound way of hedging against fashion's volatility but that doesn't make it any less axiomatic for Magee1866 to supply tweeds to interior designers. Being naturally resistant to fading, staining, wrinkling, and fire, wool has always been an excellent fiber for use in commercial or residential properties. To interior designers, the patterns and hues of tweeds may serve as contrasting or advancing colors. Tweeds can also perfectly complement any design theme of a space or simply serve to dampen light. From decorative accessories like slipcovers to furniture upholstery, from curtains and wallcoverings to area carpeting and runners, there is a sundry of applications imaginable. Nonetheless, seasoned manufacturers like Magee1866 will first devote diligent research and development because tweeds for tailoring differ markedly from the technical specifications required for interior design.

While Magee1866's residential and commercial grade tweeds are fairly new to the market, there are obviously many other manufacturers that specialize in just those categories. The most appropriate cloth for these ultimately depends on particulars. But the cloth's weight and/or density are the most basic aspects to consider. Simple logic dictates that heavier, tightly woven material (around 17oz and 450-and-above grams per meter) is best for anything subject to constant use or exposure to friction like rugs and furniture or car upholstery, or anything else used at public settings. The same material may also be ideal as curtains if the space could benefit from holding in heat. Conversely, lighter weight tweeds (from 3 up to 14oz, from 100 to 330 grams per meter) may be used for anything from simple embellishments and trims to small items like bolsters and for upholstering furniture that will be exposed to less stress.

But unsurprisingly, many in the shelter industry don't refer to the material as tweed probably because the word is more closely related to clothing. Then there's the matter of how, aside from Harris Tweed, the precise constitution of tweed can be somewhat ambiguous. Ever since synthetic fibers like nylon, viscose, and polyester, and natural ones like cotton came to be blended with wool, the kinds of tweeds that could be manufactured became innumerable. And to most of the general public, the only tweed they know is Harris. Still, more and more interior designers and fabric manufacturers have started using the name to avail of its implied history and status.

- - - - - - - -

In Seattle, Washington, Glant Textiles has been producing two collections a year of contemporary fabrics for the interior design market since it was founded by its CEO Gary Glant in 1976. There are no prints to be found among its current two thousand varieties, which are predominantly woven out of natural fibers. For that reason, Glant has earned industry-wide renown in effectively evincing sophistication and luxury purely through color, pattern, and texture. Its constructions have been utilized and installed by leading interior designers for the Ritz Carlton and Hôtel de Crillon in Paris, the Giorgio Armani store in New York, the homes of celebrities like Oprah Winfrey, Martha Stewart, and Jennifer Anniston, as well as in other opulent abodes, hotels, restaurants, private aircrafts and yachts around the world. In 2017, Italian wing chairs upholstered in Glant tweeds appeared in the industry's premier publication Elle Decor for a spread on the Stephan Jones-decorated loft of San Francisco art dealer Frank Mill.

Gary started in the business with a chain of fabric stores before taking a headlong dive into creating his own fabrics. Laden with design ideas he wanted translated into real materials, he went in search of a mill. He was set on finding one in Italy where for centuries regions like Biella and Prato were famous as textile centers in woolen, while Como specialized in silk, and Vercelli in cotton, silk, and wool. There are close to two thousand family-owned mills in just this area of Northern Italy. After traversing countless miles and knocking on as many doors, Gary chanced upon a small mill in Lombardy, in the city of Bergamo, where many manufacturing companies had cropped up thanks in part to being a scant fifty to sixty kilometers from the country's fashion capital, Milan. There, on via Buratti was a mill called Texital, which had been producing material since the 1950s for leading furniture makers such as Giorgetti and Moroso. There was instant *simpatia* between Gary and the mill's owner Carlo Peri, who seemed to instinctively grasp whatever concept the enterprising American proposed.

With the materials produced at Texital, Glant textiles were quickly put into use by interior designers for sofas, chairs, sectionals, headboards, ottomans, banquettes, beddings, pillows, drapery, and wall coverings. Gary's fabrics garnered much of that initial attention for their architectural disposition and the potency of its textures. But when he began to dabble in colors, thereby revealing deftness in handling their nuances, everyone in the industry began to sit up and take serious notice.

An art lover and avid collector, Gary has always had a heightened color sense, which he's used with canniness by distilling design and color inspirations from his everyday surroundings in the Pacific Northwest, his stays in Bergamo, and his travels to Bali, Venice, and other far-flung destinations. And it's a skill he's inculcated in his son Adam. The earliest memories Adam has of Bergamo are peppered by languorous bicycle rides along the countryside and hanging out with his father at the mill, learning how to pick out the right colors for fabrics. The family was there so often they even took up temporary residence in the 1990s. More than a second home, Adam says, "Bergamo, and indeed the mill, are very much integral to who I am." So much so that although he graduated from the University of Washington School of Law and spent a number of years handling international corporate transactions and mergers and acquisitions for the Seattle office of multinational law firm Perkins Coie, Adam officially joined Glant Textiles in 2011 as president to work alongside Gary.

"The possibility of my becoming part of the business had come up in family conversations often enough before, but the decision was solely my own." Adam confides, "Frankly, while I was with the law firm, I was always going to the mill in Italy for my vacations anyway. And I spent them pitching in at the mill. After a while, whenever I was at my law practice, I realized how much I missed being immersed in all that creativity that I had grown up with. And I was also envious of my corporate clients who devoted themselves to growing businesses they were proud of, while as just their counsel, I was merely moving from client to client." He pauses before continuing, "These touchable attributes of the textile industry, specifically the high end segment of the industry, which is our niche, is something that I do so enjoy. In a world that is increasingly digital, I love how not only can you see the beauty of these patterns and colors, but you can take what we make into your hands and feel its quality. I have been involved in the family business my entire life, whether officially or unofficially. It is and always will be part of me."

Gary felt similarly in the way the mill has always been a part of Glant. When Texital's owner died in the late 1990s without an heir to whom the business could have been bequeathed, he couldn't bear the possibilities of the mill either being bought by an indifferent corporate entity or suffer an ignoble shutdown. Not only would it have meant losing a vital resource for Glant Textiles, but it may have resulted in unemployment for everyone who worked there. Gary says, Texital's manager Giuseppe Della Vite with whom he's worked since the 1970s, is like a brother to him. It was an easy and logical decision for Glant Textiles to acquire the mill. Adam says, "We have worked shoulder to shoulder with these people for years. They are our extended family. My father couldn't turn his back on them, besides which one would be hard pressed to find new people with their level of craftsmanship and skills. And, you can't put a price on the dedication they give to what we all do together." Though it was all along anyway, the mill formally became part of Glant Textiles in 1998, making the brand one of very few American interiors and furniture fabric companies with its very own mill.

Adam says, "Working closely with our team at the mill has always been invaluable in so many ways. Through the years, we've gained a thorough understanding of the entire production cycle from selecting the right fibers in making innovative yarns and the dyeing process to the kinds of constructions our looms are capable of weaving." And Glant's proven track record among professional decorators and furniture makers generally precludes the need to direct those capabilities toward custom designs. "Because of our vast ranges of colors and textures it is a very rare exception that a designer needs to have something customized," says Adam. "But on those occasions, we are able to satisfy requests. The minimum quite depends on many factors including quantities of yarns for custom dye baths, as well as yarns required for warps." He adds, "Most interior designers and furniture manufacturers already know what they are looking for before they come to us. They may have also already either gone through the swatches, our website, or our Instagram account."

Peter Sandel, who frequently works with Glant Textiles, verifies that supposition. At his studio, this highly sought-after New York interior designer has several of Glant's swatch books within arm's reach for quick reference. He says, "Established relationships with my vendors and workrooms are indispensable to bringing an interior design project to successful fruition. Knowing their fortes and dependability in executing things in a timely and effective manner go a long way in how I can successfully do my job." From a public space to the most private of domains, his job is creating the exquisite stages, and by extension the prevailing atmosphere, in which everyday lives ensue. In Peter's case, these are often inhabited by the sort of power brokers and creative luminaries who appear on Fortune 500 lists or Page Six.

But Peter is well acquainted with people in power. His previous occupation was as a Washington DC lobbyist. Although interior design seems a far cry from lobbying, the finesse Peter must have mastered while wending his way around Capitol Hill's byzantine machinations has evidently been beneficial in dealing with New York's carriage trade. But the real guiding influence of his life has to be his late mother Lauren Sandel. "She was my first and most talented creative inspiration," Peter openly professes. Although Texas born, Peter grew up in repeatedly changing backdrops because the family had to relocate every few years according to his father's obligations as a Navy pilot and aide to an admiral. For twelve years, the Sandels moved around the Middle East, Europe, and throughout the United States. Yet each pitstop, Peter recalls, was made consistently tranquil and homey by Lauren, a native Floridian whose father had emigrated to the US from Scotland. "She was a dutiful military housewife to my Dad. Wherever we were, she made it feel settled and well designed. To this day, I have this pair of vintage saddle seats she got from Bahrain as a treasured reminder of her eye for the extraordinary."

It was Lauren's untimely passing from breast cancer in 2008 that provoked in Peter an abrupt reassessment of his priorities. He left politics, convinced he would be better off in pursuit of something creatively engaging. He was already living in New York and decided to stay in the city because by then he says, "I couldn't imagine calling any place other than the West Village home". His instinct proved judicious when he began working for the eminent architect Peter Marino, principally known for creating the stores of top drawer fashion brands including Chanel, Dior, Louis Vuitton, Calvin Klein, Ermenegildo Zegna and Fendi. But grateful and gratified as he was by the experience, Peter was eager to find his own design "voice" and build a name for himself.

He left Marino and attended the New York School of Interior Design while setting up his own boutique firm. Demonstrating his agility in designing everything from classic to minimalist, from bohemian to mid century modern, he quickly accumulated projects. He describes his work as being "refined yet relatable", layering in details that "harmonize client interest, contemporary aesthetics, and classical references." So while Peter refuses to be locked into a signature style, it is mostly in personal endeavors, such as designing vignettes for fundraising charity events, where glimpses of his predispositions materialize. A leather club chair will betray traces of Lone Star state bravado. Allusions to the sunny climes of Jupiter Island or Palm Beach may be deciphered in the candy colored throw pillows. There will be plants and beach related curios, both of which were special to his mother.

In Peter's professional capacity, however, the client's wishes are what matters. He explains, "Residential interior design, specifically, is a collaborative process on a highly personal level. It often starts with a client coming to me with images and a bunch of ideas gleaned from social media and magazine clippings. They may show me some artwork bought during their travels, or a piece of family furniture. And sure these things can give you an idea of what they like but I usually look beyond those, and instead attentively listen for verbal cues, emotional triggers, stories that get these people excited. I also study their wardrobes and figure out how they want the world to perceive them through their outward appearance."

Peter says, "Working with an interior designer gives someone advantages unavailable to the general public such as shopping the trade showrooms. While online sourcing is efficient, there's nothing like giving the client a chance to touch the fabrics, get the feel of a drawer pull, or run their fingers along the polish and grain of a wood finish." He continues, "We're also expected to anticipate everything from how the space is going to be used, the regional climates of where the project is located. All those affect the final design. When that ongoing dialogue with a client has been set, then we can move forward with schematics, presentations, procurement, and project management."

Based on his experience, he finds that while clients count on him to come up with the design, they will all want these spaces to reflect their stories. "I've yet to work with a client who doesn't have a personal narrative they want expressed through design. And the more forthcoming they are with me, the more actively participating they become, the better. As we learn about one another, trust is built on both sides." Without question, it's a relationship akin to that of a man and his tailor in which the mutual quest can endow the end result with precious significance. Says Peter, "The main objective is for the client and I to reach a consensus that stylistically feels authentic to who they are. Sure, creature comforts are important but they have to be relevant to those who will live and hopefully flourish in these surroundings."

But Peter makes clear that a shared vision is merely a prelude to the lengthy process itself. "Once the ideas in my mind start brewing, it won't switch off until the project is long over." What invariably tops his to-do list is choosing appropriate fabrics. He says, "I do tend to start with the textiles I'm inspired to use, many of which are wool-based because of the myriad compositions, durability, and ease of cleaning. Depending on the space, it can be a 100% wool rug that grounds the room, or as the foundational material for a blended upholstery like combining the strength of a wool woven with the sheen of silk or the hand of cashmere." According to him, inspecting materials with clients contributes to their education on how the qualities of certain fabrics make them viable in dissimilar ways and according to a given situation. "Everything we use becomes investment pieces toward a better way of living. Helping our clients choose elements that are easy to maintain, adds life to the piece or space, and value to their pocketbooks, those are responsibilities we don't take lightly," he says.

Tweed, says Peter, checks many of the boxes he looks for in most circumstances. "The versatility of tweed works well in both traditional and contemporary settings. It delivers a refined and crisp finish for upholstery, holds its form while looking and feeling bespoke, not at all mass produced." But with the countless varieties out there, he reiterates how critical it is to source from reputable textile houses. And any interior designer worth consulting should well know which brands make what kind of materials, their run capabilities, and in certain cases, which ones are willing to weave an original pattern on commission. He elaborates, "Custom design often comes down to a numbers game of what makes sense to the fabric maker for a small batch order. Commissioned orders for say 10-20 yards of fabric to reupholster a single chair or sofa are more demanding and costly to produce. Luxury commercial design projects, on the other hand, can ask for detailed product runs specific to the job since these are routinely bulk orders and more profitable for the textile company."

His picks of manufacturers for high-end woolen textiles like tweeds, prima alpaca, silks, and luxury linens include Glant as well as London-based brands Holland & Sherry (Est. 1836) and Claremont (Est. 1931). "I prefer working with vendors who employ small European textile manufacturers, especially those family-owned mills that still craft on old world looms. They can produce new lines that carry with them the mill's rich back story." And that, he insists, can be consequential to the result. "There's a spirit in those fabrics that come through when we use them, for example, to reupholster a client's existing furniture. The piece may already have meaning to the owner but that can be underscored, deep-ened, or revitalized by bringing in the handsome hand of a well-made tweed."

Visual appeal and utility aside, the environmental impact of choos-ing tweed has taken on greater import as of late says Peter. "We want our clients to enjoy the pieces we create for them for many years to come. Buying better or reinventing a vintage or antique piece with new upholstery is also an investment in the environment, eliminating the need to purchase mass produced furniture that all too soon ends up in a landfill." Peter adds, "Fortunately, recycled wool makes up a large percentage of fabrics from companies that are dedicated to both inno-vation and sustainability. And consumers now expect options that are both beautiful and mindful of their carbon footprint." And he opines that more companies will be doing business in ways that help preserve both flora and fauna while respecting the indigenous ways of life in the regions from which raw materials are harvested. "It's the next chapter everyone in the industry is paying very close attention to and we're very much looking forward to the day these become the norm."

- - - - - - - -

Logically, a smaller mill is apt to harness its assets with more econ-omy. At Glant, Adam confirms that they are very careful not to reck-lessly waste anything. "We try to use every bit of material we have. It's simply the efficient and effective thing to do. Everything that is woven is used," he says. "And since they are all manufactured to our stipula-tions, the quantity of yarn spun is exactly what is needed, which is then colored with the right amount of dye, and then woven for the yardage that was required." Any unavoidable excess fibers or yarns are also put to good use in design development, which is a never ending process at Glant.

Gary and Adam are both actively involved in designing Glant's Spring collection, which unfurls in January, followed by the Autumn collection at the end of August. "But we don't stick to a regimented schedule when it comes to designing. It's more like a free flowing process that happens all year round." The father and son can begin on any given day with discussions about something that inspires them from nature, architecture, fashion, food, art, travel, or whatever else that may have caught their eye. "Then we'll talk about how this could be interpreted into fabric. And there's no real beginning or end to this. We just keep going at it." Adam says he and his father will very often, though not always, agree on a design direction. But once they arrive at the mill, they will also hear from the in-house designers, who've independently come up with ideas of their own. And they will all freely bounce these concepts off each other until they come up with a sensible game plan. "We welcome everyone's input because we trust each other's expertise and design sense," he says. "Then, we'll confer with our skilled technicians on how to realize those planned concepts and we'll tweak them as necessary."

Final proof, however, is in the weaving. And it's at the looms, during experimentations with the yarns and colors when any excess materials may be incorporated. "We could be working on a single yarn basketweave or a complex mélange, so the types of yarn we end up using depend on what we envisioned for that article." But even those trial runs that don't wind up in the season's collection will still be cataloged into the mill's archives for possible use in the future. That future, incidentally, involves a bit of 'turnabout is fair play'. Just as fashion manufacturers like Magee1866 are entering the home sector, Glant Textiles is diversifying into fashion with the Adam Glant collection of woven fabric and leather bags. Adam says, "We just launched and I hope to expand into various colors and styles, all using our fabric, of course. And without giving anything away, I anticipate there will eventually be tweeds, as I plan on representing a wide variety of Glant textiles with the bags." As accessories go, bags aren't the only ones for which tweed has found use. Another category in which artful collaborations between buzzy brands and major manufacturers prove the cloth's seemingly limitless versatility is footwear.

- - - - - - - -

Something is amiss on Boston's Clearway Street. In this aggressively gentrified yet otherwise innocuous neighborhood, there's a convenience store where the paper towels, boxes of detergent, and canned goods pressed against the windows look odd somehow. With vaguely familiar logos, they appear to be the same products ordinarily found at such places; except these brand names don't exist. Inside, it looks like other such stores lodged at the corner of city streets everywhere, overflowing with junk food, beverages, and lottery scratchers. But somewhere in the back is a deceptively looking Snapple merchandising refrigerator that's in actuality the sliding door into the real shop called, what else, "Bodega".

By now, every serious sneakerhead, streetwear or menswear aficionado has made the pilgrimage to this bastion of kicks, hoodies, T shirts and assorted fashions for men and women. Despite widespread acclaim, Bodega's steely grip on its too-cool cred is well earned for still brazenly ignoring the commercial impulses others would find irresistible. Another brand with the name recognition of Bodega would've franchised the hell out of the concept already. Not for friends Jay Gordon, Dan Notola, and Oliver Mak, the gentlemen who conceived the store in 2006.

Indeed when the three friends got together back then, they dreamt this up as retail meets speakeasy (minus peephole grille, secret password, bathtub gin, or bootleg liquor). There were no splashy ads or gaudy marketing promotions either – just hushed word of mouth and patiently building awareness among like minded folks. Oliver says, "From the very start we were more invested in creating this underground 'performance art' type vibe around it than actually selling products. We wanted to stoke an emotional sense of discovery and gather a community of people who felt as passionately as we did about art and fashion." It was also hoped they could ultimately foster creative camaraderie and at the same time potentially incubate fledgling brands into something monetarily feasible for the designers.

Expectedly, Boston's savvy shoppers had no trouble finding their way to the "hidden in plain sight" store. Sure, there was that initial lure of curiosity and the self-satisfaction of being in-the-know. But because the trio had a talent for curating the items that ended up on their shelves, streetwear fans began swarming the store. And they all found the manner by which Bodega collated its streetwear, sneakers and other footwear was guided as much by art as fashion. The pieces themselves are made all the more covetable for their limited edition runs. Talk of the store got around quickly, not just in Boston, but all over the world. Everyone was soon urging everyone else to come for the schtick, stay for the merch. Oliver freely admits that Boston is hardly a "fashion city" and that it was opening up shop in Los Angeles in 2018 that was a game changer for them. He says, "The LA store gave us more mainstream exposure and attracted many celebrity sneakerheads." And while they've done pop ups like one at Miami's Art Basel and another in Tokyo (originally slated for three months but so successful it ran for a year), they're in no rush to open another store.

In 2012, tweed became a pivotal part of one of Bodega's many memorable pieces: the Country Brogue shoes crafted in collaboration with designer Mark McNairy. As the creative director for five years at J. Press, McNairy was responsible for a welcome update of that brand's Ivy League-centric pieces. After successfully venturing out on his own, he's attracted a following for modern footwear and casual menswear collections that dovetail so neatly into the Bodega sensibility their collaboration was a slam dunk from the get go. The Bodega x Mark McNairy Country Brogue was a smartly fresh take on the brogue shoes featuring quarters and toe cap in caramel-colored full grain waxed leather, split across and accented by a vamp of herringbone tweed.

The use of tweed in this unexpected context lent the shoes the strongly visual and modern flair for which the Bodega boys and McNairy are celebrated. But it's almost certain few of the people who bought those shoes were truly aware of how clever the idea was. Brogues, or wingtips as they are called in the US, with their perforated toe caps are mostly remembered for their popularity during the Jazz

Age. In the 1920s stepping out to swing clubs could only be done in style with a pair of gleaming two-tone brogues. But the name itself is said to have been derived from 16th century Gaelic Ireland (*bróg*) and Scotland (*bròg*) in reference to "shoes". Brogues were worn as country footwear and ideally matched with tweed garments during the 18th century. The perforations weren't meant to be merely decorative, rather to let water seep out of the shoes after the wearer has treaded sodden ground or stepped into bogs.

The Bodega boys would once again dip their toes into tweed in 2015 with another collaboration. Partnered with Reebok, the British-turned-American brand now a subsidiary of German sporting goods giant Adidas, Bodega created a pair of sneakers called "Inferno". Oliver recounts, "They were manufactured by Reebok but designed entirely in-house by Marvin Bynoe and Randy Price. They came up with two striking versions with either a purple or orange accent. But both colorways sported dark brown tweed quarter panels supported by premium nubuck suede in brown and tan." For all their unusual qualities however, these sneakers weren't the first to feature tweed. A good decade prior, a major brand had already incorporated Harris Tweed into a line of sneakers. And Dr. Martens, the British boots brand, founded by Dr. Klaus Märtens after WWII, has also incorporated Harris Tweed into some of its footwear. But it's the sincerity behind everything Bodega makes that sets their products apart and endears them to the somewhat obsessive sneakerhead community. That subculture dedicated to obtaining and collecting sneakers of significant genesis emerged in the 1980s and has only grown exponentially in the past few decades. Like other forms of fandom, members of this community have their own standards by which certain items are prized. In many instances, their interests overlap with streetwear and menswear fans, all of whom designate authenticity as the most meaningful of factors. Oliver says, "You can't 'manufacture' authenticity. Tweed and other heritage fabrics are part of our DNA. And our constant explorations in re-contextualizing classic materials into sportswear will always make them essential to us." He adds, "Even using them in blocked mixed media is very much a Bodega look."

The looks and influences cherished by Bodega's principals such as Northern Soul music and counterculture are clearly imprinted on the store. But the premium Oliver and company places on Bodega's cult-like status stems from having been schooled in all things menswear by their mentor Bobby Garnett (1950-2016) a.k.a. Bobby from Boston. "Everything we know we learned from Bobby," Oliver says. "I learned how to tie a bow tie from him." Garnett, who was also called "Bert" by friends, was a true connoisseur of all things vintage and an adored local fixture. His very first vintage store, "Uptown Strutters Ball" opened in the mid 1970s on Commercial Street in Provincetown, MA. His last, "Bobby from Boston", on South End started as an appointment-only showroom but became a retail store in the 1990s. This is where he spent his remaining years, wheelchair-bound but ever convivial and always regaling customers and visitors like Oliver with stories and advice on style. "Up until the end Bobby was active. He still traveled for his business and was always so welcoming and friendly," Oliver says. "It was that sense of community Bobby built around his store that we've tried to recreate at Bodega."

Throughout his career, Garnett was the Mohammed to whom mountains came. Costume designers, production companies, and fashion big wigs like Ralph Lauren, Marc Jacobs, Tommy Hilfiger, and Tom Ford all came seeking specific items or sparks of inspiration from his cache of vintage items. And if the designers couldn't make the trip themselves, emissaries were dispatched to the store. Packed to the rafters with paraphernalia, the place can be overwhelming. But many don't mind. Among those racks and racks of jeans, coats, and sweaters, walls of hats, stacks of luggage, lunch boxes, thermoses, roller skates, and US postal office issued mailbags is a find that someone will tell someone else was a treasure they unearthed at Bobby's. Of course, here there be tweeds. He's supplied garments and other items for period films like the Sam Mendes' 2002 Depression-era picture "Road to Perdition", and biopics such as Ron Howard's 2001 "A Beautiful Mind" about math genius and

Princeton University professor John Forbes Nash Jr., and Martin Scorsese's 2004 "The Aviator" about Howard Hughes. When the South End location was turned into a retail store, the showroom - where all the good stuff was kept - moved forty miles north to a 5,000 square foot space in Lynn, MA. Much to the relieved appreciation of many, Garnett's daughter Jessica Carrion decided to continue her late father's business by consolidating all operations to the Bobby's of Boston Lynn warehouse.

- - - - - - - -

Antiques are big business. But there is an equally lucrative market for less expensive items like clothing and everyday personal effects from bygone eras. Dealers, like Bobby from Boston, exist all over the world. In the UK, John Morgan who describes himself, with tongue firmly in cheek, as "junkman to the gentry" has a store with an onsite "museum" in Dorset along the coast of the English Channel. He buys, sells, and rents out props and costumes to private individuals, collectors, stylists, and film and television property masters for sets, shoots or simply the personal pleasure of owning a piece of history. While his inventory has expanded substantially since he started in the 1980s and he now specializes more in military uniforms and gear, John started this vocation with mostly civilian garments and seeking out well-made tweed suits.

During the 1980s, while still attending the all-boys' Merchant Taylors' School (Est. 1620) near Liverpool, John was already an astutely enterprising young fellow. Growing up at the seaside resort town of Southport, he frequented the local charity and thrift shops, and worked his way around the used clothes aisles as well as into the good graces of the elderly volunteers. If he couldn't afford to buy an item, he cajoled them into setting it aside until his return. Whatever he bought, he sold to his classmates. The ones that generated the most sales were suits or coats in styles popularized by the nattily-dressed bands of the New Romantic music culture so widely imitated at the time, or classics seen in the televised adaptation of the Evelyn Waugh (1903-1966) classic

"Brideshead Revisited". Regularly rummaging through racks and bins quickly taught John how to assess the merits, conditions, and sizes of garments.

"Harris Tweed jackets were so popular and complete tweed suits were the holy grail," he says. "The bespoke tailored ones with waistcoats were always at the top of my wish list because there were always buyers for those. Next in order were garments from the more prestigious provincial outfitters for gentlemen. In the case of the Northwest of England, which had been enormously prosperous during the 19th and most of the 20th centuries, those from Watson Prickard along with Mander & Allender of Liverpool were great," he explains. "These places had provided the mercantile and professional classes of the region their city suits, shirts and accessories for the week, the tweed and corduroy clothing for wearing at the golf club, and evening suits for white or black tie events, which were the social networking glue of those days." Then, there was the bottom of the pile: off-the-peg outfitters' clothing from the likes of Burton, Moss Bros., and John Collier. "Cheap and easy to buy, more difficult to sell," he says.

By 1987 his self-described "accidental business" was thriving. He was supplying to some of the most elegant vintage menswear shops, one of which was Jeremy Hackett's in Chelsea. Today Hackett produces his own garments, but he started with well-selected second-hand clothes acquired from Portobello flea markets and suppliers like John. "Each week I drove down from Liverpool with my old MG Midget full of kit to sell to stores like Hackett's," he says. He would then leave with an empty trunk and often, to his chagrin, an empty wallet, having spent all his earnings in London. It was through Hackett that John met someone who worked at Polo Ralph Lauren and shortly thereafter he began providing the label with luggage and riding boots for its window and store displays. He adds, "Their design department also Hoovered up old cricket jerseys, sporting blazers, and particularly tweed overcoats as inspiration for next season's range." John confirms that many are the fashion, costume, and set designers who regularly rummage for genuine vintage pieces or stray but fabulous buttons and beads at his own hunting grounds along the rows of stalls at flea markets from Les Puces (more formally known as the Marché aux Puces de Clignancourt) in Paris to good old Portobello Road and the Old Spitalfields markets in London.

In due course, John was buying and selling by the van load, and purchasing privately from "estate effects and the finest of British country houses". He once lucked out on the entire wardrobe of a former equerry to HM King Edward VIII. He chuckles, "The result of attempting to keep up with one of the best-dressed men in history must have resulted in bankruptcy for the late officer." John's dealings with fashion companies weren't his only high profile coups. He has also supplied items for major television and motion picture projects. His antique luggage, overnighters, and steamer trunks appeared on many of the train platform scenes throughout the Harry Potter series of films. He did the same for all the comings and goings of the fictitious "Downton Abbey" Crawleys in the widely popular ITV-PBS sudser.. Through it all, tweed has been a constant. "I enjoy deer-stalking in the Highlands of Scotland clad in the stuff on wild winter days." And John offers a bit of wise counsel, "The smell of decent tweed is gorgeous and a man would do well to test this on any potential partner by wearing tweed at the earliest part of getting to know someone. If they don't agree then the relationship will not flourish!"

VII

One More Reason to Keep Believing

When deciding what to wear, a garment's design (or designer), function, and colors are normally the motivating factors. Price comes into play if it's a purchase. But pertinent to how a garment is going to be assembled, the people behind needle and thread have to give commensurate thought to the material and its inherent properties. Weight, for example, (expressed in ounces per square yard or grams per square meter) can indicate the density of the weave and therefore the pliability of the material, how it will drape, and under what conditions the garment may best be worn. All told, there are more than a few reasons why it is often best to start with the cloth.

Thumbing through books of fabric swatches and picking out the one cloth with which to have a suit made can be quite daunting. The plenitude of choices and considerations may easily cause paralyzing indecision. Yet this not only affords an ideal way of assessing if a certain material is visually appealing, but perhaps even more importantly, it is an excellent way to determine how the fabric feels against skin. In the peculiar patois of fashion people, describing this tactile sensation as the "hand" of a fabric means exactly that: how the fabric feels in one's hand. Certainly an extent of subjectivity is to be expected. One man's "crisp" may be someone else's "bristly". But professionals gauge varying reactions by touch along standards of rigidity, thread count, twist, hairiness, softness, and friction. Thus a material may be said to have a soft or coarse or smooth hand, and so on.

Of course when Will fixed his sights on the Dashing Tweeds brand, his only means of appraisal was viewing computer screen pixels. It did help that Dashing Tweeds had already earned its reputation for quality. So he was able to scroll through the images of the brand's fabrics on its website and trust that he could make a choice based solely on its self-proclaimed "unashamedly directional" designs. Those designs are wholly Kirsty's, though Guy says he does give his input. He admits, "I don't actually know that much technical stuff about weaving, which directly impacts the designs. But Kirsty and I work very well together and we always agree on color combinations. So we sit and talk about ideas and create yarn color combinations together." After she hand looms swatches of their concepts, they can better review and refine the prototypes before going into production. He reveals, "We almost always end up with some wonderful patterns so the hardest part is selecting just a few we send off to be manufactured by the mills."

Aside from the assortment of Lumatwill-based tweeds, the brand offers specialized yarns including Lurex, rubber, silk, linen and Japanese cotton. Kirsty creates some eight new designs for each of two seasonal collections a year. During the Spring-Summer season, Australian Merino wools are used while heavier British wools dominate the label's Autumn-Winter collection. The collection themes - culled from obscure Sci-Fi novels and television shows and adventurous Arctic expeditions - are also obviously coded by Guy's parallel interests in both the practical and the fanciful. Recently, Guy's love for music was also represented when Dashing Tweeds collaborated with Gordon Millings the son of famous Beatles tailor Dougie Millings "using some of the original patterns he cut for the Fab Four".

From the available selections on the Dashing Tweeds website, Will shortlisted his preferences to the Brave Explorer, the Ben Loyal, and the Dashing Explorer. In the end, it came down to the ochre, copper, green, blue, and plum-patterned Dashing Explorer cloth with its barely-there pinstripes. At Alan Flusser, Andrew says, "We found the Lumatwill cloth intriguing in the dark and tasteful in the light, and proceeded to order a length of the material from London." Will was confident this breathable material was the best choice and would adapt well to both mild and cold weather, "perfect for walks and cycling".

- - - - - - - -

Not too long ago, if someone attired in tweed were to come serenely gliding down a street on a bicycle, heads would've turned. But it's occurring with such increasing frequency that it's less the attention grabbing spectacle it used to be. At some point this could even become more of an everyday sight. Many cities are fostering cycling not just for its health and fitness benefits but as a short term way of easing traffic congestion and a long range effort in stemming environmental problems caused by polluting carbon emissions. A 2018 mobility study estimates that 460,000 cycling trips take place every day in New York City. London reports around 580,000. While no one is arguing that Lycra better handles the practical exigencies of competitive racing, to the average cyclist, tweeds offer a sartorially kinder and superior alternative. And that reflective yarn in Dashing Tweed's Lumatwill cloth provides the same safeguard feature found in some Lycra outfits that glow against the beams of oncoming automobile headlights.

So while Guy has allocated more of his store's shelf space to cloth, he hasn't entirely given up on making several ready-to-wear tweed pieces aimed at cyclists. Their cuts are often guided by Guy's personal experiences of biking around London since his fondness for cycling helped shape Dashing Tweeds in the first place. He says, "I've enjoyed cycling ever since I was a child. In the 1980s, my brother signed us both up as cycle couriers during the school holidays. We used to earn a lot of money because there were very few couriers back then." And when his own kids were younger, he would routinely take them to school by strapping them all securely to a four-seater custom bike. "It was like a circus every morning," he laughs. When word got to him about the first

London Tweed Run in 2009, he didn't hesitate to sign up for it. "I'm not sure who told me about it. But I was going out often and it was definitely on the grapevine. I went wearing the original cycle suit from the first piece of cloth Kirsty and I worked on."

- - - - - - - -

The original Tweed Run in London was founded by Ted Young-Ing as something of a lark. Ted's career at that point had included working as campaign art director for the YSL Beauté brands when it was still under the leadership of Domenico De Sole and Tom Ford for Gucci Group NV. Ted had also served as art director for the bicycle accessories manufacturer Brooks England. On how the Tweed Run was conceived, he recounts, "I was in a thrift shop in Glasgow when I happened upon these brilliant plus-fours tweeds and decided to buy them on the spot. But after trying them on back in London, I had a momentary attack of buyer's remorse when I thought I couldn't possibly just wear them out on a casual bike ride." Instead, he came up with a fun idea of getting some people together to put on their tweeds for a ride around town. "I'm a keen cyclist so I thought I could make it like a pub crawl on bikes and use that as an excuse to wear my tweeds." He mentioned this get-together on an online cycling forum, thinking he could probably tempt maybe thirty people at the most to join him. To his astonishment, within a week of having posted his suggestion, 200 people had signed up.

"That first year was a guerilla event," Ted says. "We didn't have a permit." But people came in droves, preening in their tweeds, bowties, caps, bowlers, and some sporting extravagant handlebar mustaches. There were even one or two penny farthings in the crowd. Ted confesses to being simply flabbergasted that first year by both the huge turnout and the outpouring of enthusiasm and joy from the participants. Of course now he's become more than a casual fan of tweed. He says, "It is a downright amazing material. You can stick it with a pencil and it will go all the way through to the other side. Then, you adjust it a bit and it's still perfectly intact." He is likewise impressed by its longevity and value as something that can be treasured. He's since had his own tweed suit made in a red, black, and orange pattern.

Guy remembers having a blast at the Tweed Run, "We all met right outside of Vogue in Hanover Square and biked around town causing a bit of chaos when traffic got in the way. It was great fun with all sorts of people who were either more seriously into cycling or more into tweed. There were stops in the park for tea and entertainment such as bands playing music on saws and violins, and people dancing to old records." No one involved had any clue at how far more widespread the interest was in reveling in the past. Guy says that concurrent to the Tweed Run, a big retro party scene in the East End of London was also organically forming, feeding into a vibe very similar to the cycling revelry. "It was attracting the same crowd of fun Londoners, people who were either in fashion or just enjoyed dressing up. Tailors and folks from Savile Row such as Paul (Abraham) who loves 70's vintage were at these gatherings." Regardless of their own proclivities, they all came to bask in the fun.

Ted's Tweed Run, meanwhile, had proven to be more than a successful fluke that by the following year, he thought it pragmatic to get organized. Jacqui Shannon, a PR woman who was in attendance the year before, came onboard to help. They applied for and received an official permit from the city, capped off the tally to 500 cyclists, and had ticket sales apportioned to charitable causes such as the London Cycling Campaign. Each successive year also managed to attract larger crowds and more participating companies and organizations. Guy says Dashing Tweeds "sponsored some of our reflective Lumatwill cycling tweeds on several occasions. They used the fabric to make sashes, caps, and accessories for the marshals." The Dashing Tweeds cap was decisively popular with its handsome yet no less practical design of an extended brim to ward off rain and a deeper back panel for a firmer fit.

Shortly thereafter, other cities, organizations and promoters were ringing up Ted to get his permission to inaugurate their own local tweed runs. Officially affiliated as well as unsanctioned tweed rides began cropping up everywhere: Madrid, Stuttgart, Copenhagen, Sydney, Beijing, along with Kansas City, Philadelphia, Washington DC, and

Denver in the US. Some British brands also took part in some of these overseas festivities. Barbour (Est 1894) was a sponsor of the Poseidonion Grand Hotel's 4th annual Tweed Run in Spetses where hotel guests, tourists, and a handful of Spetsiots cheerfully took to the narrow cobblestoned streets in their smartest tweed outfits. In 2011, Ralph Lauren's people reached out to Ted to hold a New York Tweed Run (effectively supplanting the earlier Big Apple Tweed Ride) under the banner of their Rugby Ralph Lauren (RRL) line. Conceived in 2004, the RRL line was sporty if a trifle jejune, and basically a diluted version of Polo. Organized with care and supported by all the trappings of a full-scale marketing hoopla, the RRL Tweed Run was going to be a major event. Until it wasn't. After effusive online publicity via GQ, Racked, and Refinery29, it was cancelled at the last minute, reportedly because the police force required to manage the crowd was re-tasked further downtown to the Occupy Wall Street protest that was going on at the time. Organizers presented a brave face and requested everyone to gather at the RRL store in University Place instead for food and entertainment. The brand never did get around to holding another official Tweed Run and RRL itself was quietly discontinued in 2013.

Other cities fared much better with their tweed runs. Ted lent a hand when he could and went so far as to take part in the first Tweed Run Tokyo. "It was held in conjunction with Tokyo Fashion Week," relates Ted. "It wasn't as mobbed as London but it was still a hit. By their second year they had 150 participants." He was also fascinated by the creativity of the Japanese in making the proceedings their own by coming up with ultra modern interpretations of tweed outfits: "Close fitted tailoring, unusual buttons, and beautiful details." Another uniquely Japanese feature was its rather heavy-handed PSAs with instructions to one and all on how to properly ride a bike and reminders to heed public safety. It continues to be held as part of the city's fashion week but has since added an offshoot in Oshu in the Iwate Prefecture.

After seven annual London tweed runs, however, Ted had to relocate to Berlin for his latest project as one of the founders and as creative director of AER, an artisanal perfume house. The opportunity to work on another one of his fixations was too good to pass up. "Perfume is another passion of mine. I still remember my first bottle of perfume: Geoffrey Beane's Grey Flannel." For AER he says, "We create fragrances blended by hand with 100% natural, vegan ingredients. We source from small producers who honor traditional techniques, sustainable, fair trade, and cruelty-free practices. Like Tweed!" He sold his interest in the Tweed Run brand to events planner Bourne & Hollingsworth, which is known for its retro-styled "Blitz" parties. The Tweed Run is still very popular but being in Berlin hasn't afforded Ted the chance to join its more recent editions. He says, "I still have my best tweed cycling suits. I feel confident enough now not to be too self-conscious about wearing them in public on an ordinary day. I don't have to be at the Tweed Run because I can just go wear them whenever I want."

- - - - - - - -

The Tweed Run's relevance to Tokyo Fashion Week is an obvious indication that tweeds and commerce in ethical fashion have gained traction there. Appreciation for natural materials is hardly a new phenomenon in Japan, especially since the Shinto doctrine of striving for a harmonious coexistence with nature has been around for centuries. But this recent momentum in the business of ethical fashion has alerted many international brands, particularly those in the luxury sector, to reevaluate trafficking in disposable merchandise. Try as some might to claim otherwise, climate change is no longer seen as a cause célèbre by majority of consumers. In recent years, many studies by independent groups like the Pew Research Center, as well as by environmental agencies and the fashion industry, show that shoppers have a positive impression on cotton and wool as being the most environmentally-enlightened choices in clothing. More importantly, the same studies indicate that social responsibility has become a major purchase driver as well as a mitigating factor in consumer behavior - not just in Japan but around the globe.

Despite the acute scrutiny that's been directed of late at mainland

China and South Korea as luxury markets, Japan still ranks second only to the US when it comes to spending in this category. Without a doubt, it has suffered a severe contraction during the last decade. And a reticence to online shopping in Japan has proven difficult to overcome. But among marketers, there is cause for optimism in regaining lost ground through a cogent grasp of local predispositions. One persistent obstacle though is the inability of most Westerners to comprehend the fundamental differences between their commonly individualistic thinking versus the holistic way the Japanese people see the world.

There is something generally called the triad test in which subjects are asked to choose from among three items, the two that go together. For example: "Glove", "Scarf", "Hands". Westerners are prone to classifying "glove" and "scarf" as articles of clothing and therefore compatible; whereas those with an Eastern outlook invariably select "glove" and "hands" as more contextually complementary. At the risk of belaboring the point, the Japanese are more inclined to judge value not by anything intrinsic to the object, rather in how it relates to everything else within its milieu. This inclination may not exactly be equivalent to what reportedly motivates today's affluent class in their pursuit of "experiential" additives to their shopping. But it could well be the vantage point from which luxury brands can begin to understand the Japanese as well as the rest of their market.

To the Japanese, a garment is only desirable as it pertains to such aspects as brand image and history, how it fulfills its function, how it looks in an ensemble and what that can communicate to everyone else. Even the places and circumstances in which something is made and consequently purchased matter. While academics and psychologists are better qualified to draw conclusions, would it be such a stretch to speculate a correlation between what this mindset finds favorable and why tweed found a home in Japan? Does not its mesh of yarns suggest a virtual microcosm of an interconnected world? And what are tweeds after all but nature itself having taken shape?

Merely a few years ago, an estimate was made that close to fifty percent of Harris Tweed production was still being exported to Japan annually. To appreciate how this came to be, American freelance journalist and author W. David Marx says tweed must be examined through the socio-cultural and historical perspective of a decades-long "dialogue between Japanese and American fashion". An esteemed scholar, David has spent the better part of two decades contributing dissertations on Japanese fashion, music, and culture to publications like GQ and Nylon since he moved to Tokyo in 1998. He points out that tweed was already procured directly out of Scotland in the past. But it wasn't until its odyssey east came by way of New Jersey that "it gained meaning". And perhaps more to the point it was accompanied by the other components of the Ivy League look. On its own, tweed was too much of an abstract. It was far easier to appreciate its role within the collective. Not that the appreciation happened overnight.

David singles Kensuke Ishizu (1911-2005), founder of VAN Jacket, for being Japan's most zealous advocate of the Ivy League look, having first heard of it from a Princetonian he had befriended after the second world war. In the post-war prosperity of the early 1950s, Ishizu-san's then nascent garment business was doing well with a line of sport coats. They were selling briskly to newly moneyed consumers. But societal restrictions were apparently preventing any real growth. David explains, "It was taboo for men to show interest in fashion as this implied vanity. Western suits were adopted in the early twentieth century as a modern and sober uniform taken to extremes of conformity: a single charcoal gray or navy blue suit, dark tie, white shirt, and dark shoes. And ready-to-wear was simply not acceptable." In response, Ishizu-san diverted his attention to the younger generation but he was uncertain how to proceed. His search for the right look to market took him on a trip to New York where he fortuitously recollected the friend who had told him about the Ivy League look. He decided to take a short yet no less fateful train ride to Princeton and see for himself what it was all about.

There, against the stately facade of Nassau Hall, he must have beheld young men clad in cable knit sweaters or dapper blazers, ambling across Cannon Green en route to a lecture at McCosh, a game at Dillon Gym, or crew training at Carnegie Lake. At this point, it's unlikely any of them were "PDFing" it through a course, but these Princetonians must have seemed every bit the way F. Scott Fitzgerald had described in "This Side of Paradise": "lazy and good-looking and aristocratic -you know, like a spring day". Enthralled, Ishizu-san returned to Japan armed with photographs and the abiding piety of the converted. It took him a few more years to consolidate his Ivy League look-inspired VAN collection, headlined by a near exact duplicate of a Brooks Brothers blazer, but he was definitely on the right track. He encouraged interest among Japanese youth with nothing less than propaganda at its most sartorial, regularly seeding local fashion magazines with images, illustrations, and copy touting the virtues of this style, and consequently codifying the ways of properly pulling it off.

Dogma, says David, went a long way in bestowing legitimacy to the Ivy League look in Japan, not unlike how being privy to the rules leads to becoming an expert or an insider. David elucidates, "There is a strong philosophical belief here in correct practice, generally set down by elite opinion or tradition. And everyone is expected to follow it as a sign of respect to others. I believe this is a Confucian idea/ideal in which devotion to a group or belief is gauged by how exact the ritual is conducted. So if someone identifies as an 'Ivy' devotee, the idea is that they must follow that Ivy style down to its most fundamental details. Mistakes mean carelessness, or that they haven't paid sufficient attention, or studied the rules, etc." Inevitably, this led to a "greater tyranny of details." He says, "An Ivy shirt must have a small locker loop under the collar and a center box pleat. Pocket squares had to be folded in the Ivy way. A necktie exactly seven centimeters wide. A suit can only be Ivy if the jacket had a center hooked vent, though its presence on the back made it mostly invisible. Homosocial one-upmanship brought interest in style, previously belittled as a 'feminine' pursuit, closer to 'masculine' hobbies such as car repair and sports, which are characterized by an intimate knowledge of their technical minutiae."

Oddly enough, early public opinion on the Ivy League look was firmly negative. Adults were especially vociferous, claiming that it encouraged rebellious behavior and was suitable only for delinquents. This outlook was formed largely due to the rabid following these garments had engendered among kids who belonged to the *Miyuki-zoku* (the term is a combination of the words "*Miyuki*", a street along which these young people tended to loiter, and "*zoku*", which translates as a subculture). Once school was let out, they would congregate around the Ginza neighborhood to slip out of their uniforms and into their trendiest of Ivy League outfits to socialize and hang out. Local authorities have estimated that at its peak, members of the *Miyuki-zoku* out on the streets numbered in the hundreds. While there seems to have been minimal untoward incidents, the mere sight of a daily congregation of idle teenagers inflamed fears of public disorder. Parental disapproval eased however after Ishizu-san created clothes for the hosting Japanese delegation at the Summer Olympics of 1964. When the local athletes marched into Tokyo's National Stadium in their smart ensembles of white trousers and hats, striped ties and three-button red jackets, it was a glorious moment witnessed by the entire world on the first-ever live broadcast of the games. The scene was a much-needed approbation that after the devastating second world war, Japan was once more a proud member of the international stage.

Like everywhere else, however, the Ivy League look as a trend unceremoniously faded in the 1970s, only to resurface under a new moniker by the next decade. In the US, elements of it were subsumed into the "Preppy" style. In Japan, they became part of "trad", a shortened term ripped from the headline of the bestselling 1981 book "Traditional Fashion: From Tartan Check to Button Downs" by Hisayuki Nakamuta. Perhaps predictably, "trad" would take a deeper dive into the style's original building blocks and in turn started an obsession for "*furugi*" or vintage. In keeping with the Japanese reverence for all things "*honmono*" or the genuine article, Nakamuta-san argued that authenticity in this regard can only be achieved by understanding "the clothing customs of ancient Scottish castles and golf course club houses." In "trad", tweed from Scotland finally received overdue recognition in Japan. Similarly deserved credit for pioneering the movement was given to Ishizu-san, his memory kept alive by Japan's leading fashion authorities like David.

It would be a mistake though to presume that the Japanese are simply absorbed by resurrecting the past. From the shrewdest of shoppers at Harajuku's second-hand stores to the country's top designers, from wearing "*honmono*" to upscaling materials, everyone knows taking something from the past and making it part of what's next is the objective. Today, David notes, Scottish garments and tweeds are still very much in use by trad enthusiasts and more widely worn by the public during the cooler Autumn months. But with all due deference to tweed purists, some may question why Japan imports it at all. In the 1990s, Japanese selvedge denim became one of the most coveted items in casuals, serving as a testament to the premier quality of the country's fabric manufacturing. When selvedge denim first came into the market it effectively showed how far Japan could outdistance everyone else in both the design and the quality of producing so-called American classics like jeans and hoodies. Could it not have done the same with tweed? When it comes to production, David says Japan simply never bothered to try. "Comparative to silk and cotton, Japan has never excelled at wool production," he says. "It was only in the late 19th century when the Japanese began wearing British suiting that imported wool came into use. Since then, prestige originally associated with those overseas fabric makers has become part of the cloth's appeal. Japan's wool spinners and weavers are relatively unknown, especially compared to denim manufacturers Kaihara and Kurabo. Instead of competing, the Japanese have just always imported the best of the best, which also happens to carry the true and clear sense of history important to trad clothing."

- - - - - - - -

Tradition, with all its attendant intimations of history, community, and ritual, is a crucial cornerstone for any legacy brand. But shepherding such a brand presents the question of how those traditions can be made germane to the present. Coasting on laurels long past is hardly an advisable business model. Trend forecasts are informative, sure, but they're about as prophetic as a magic 8-ball. Regrettably, nobody knows what's going to happen tomorrow. Furthermore, surviving in fashion isn't as typically Darwinian as it may be in other industries. Already fraught with a multitude of financial variables from overhead expenditures to narrow profit margins, fashion also has to negotiate frivolous accords with the general buying public that decides if brands will sink or swim. Eye-roll inducing qualifiers such as "hot" or "in" are the flimsy rafts on which a vast majority of the industry clings. Yet from among those that do flounder on its treacherous shoals, some labels like Gucci or Burberry somehow very narrowly evade certain oblivion and even manage a sensational renaissance. But how many fashion brands can actually lay claim to having been snatched from the brink by an, ahem, dyed-in-the-wool rock star?

In 1839, John Charles Cording was barely 30 years old when he opened Cordings on The Strand. Among its early offerings was the waterproof coat now generically known as a Mackintosh, after the Scottish chemist Charles Macintosh (1766-1843) who had patented his idea of placing a layer of rubber between two sheets of fabric. The extra "k" in the name of the coat came later as it gained popularity and the process of vulcanizing rubber had effectively corrected issues of its unpleasant odor and susceptibility to melting on hot days. These coats, along with fishing boots, comprised the store's weather proofing merchandise that every city gentleman never forgot to pack for a bucolic sojourn. A few decades later the business had grown enough to necessitate a move to 19 Piccadilly where it still stands today. By the 1900s, Cordings held a royal warrant. But it wasn't until the 1920s after it had augmented its catalog with waistcoats, caps, and riding boots, and finally rolled out its very own tweed jacket that Cordings earned renown for bestowing real éclat to pastoral pursuits.

The signature Cordings three-button tweed jacket - featuring spacious internal pockets, mitred edge cuffs with four (working) buttons, and a center back vent - has undergone only the most imperceptible changes through the years. Available in Harris, Shetland, or Donegal, the most sought after patterns are the House Check, Firley Herringbone, Thorner, and Barleycorn. The tweed jacket is among the five items instituted as fundamental to the Cordings brand. Another is the Covert coat, easily identifiable by the Cordings crest on the under collar as well as the four tramline stitching on its cuffs and hem. The material of the coat (choices of 14oz or 20oz) is still woven exclusively for Cordings by the Fox Brothers mill (Est. 1772) in Somerset and comes in herringbone tweed, navy, or the original "fawn" color. The latter is, incidentally, popular among riders since the unavoidable flecks of horse hair that attach themselves to the coat are made inconspicuous. Rounding out the other core pieces are the Mackintosh, corduroy and moleskin trousers, and tattersall shirts.

Through the ensuing decades Cordings' fortunes ebbed and flowed. To its credit, and arguable detriment, the shop retained its local sources and labor while other brands began resorting to cheaper offshore assets. But by the early 2000s, Cordings had become just another neglected subsidiary of a corporate entity, and its finances were in shambles. Even the addition of women's apparel in 2003 did little to boost sales. In 2005, the parent company did hire a new marketing manager called Noll Uloth, whose qualifications included serving as production director for a manufacturing company in the Midlands and working with a mail order garment business. But Noll barely had a chance to get accustomed to his new position before he realized it would take more than clever marketing to right this ship. What Cordings needed was a complete overhaul in management.

To his corporate superiors, he proposed to find a new buyer who could invest both the vital attention and cash necessary to revitalize Cordings. Noll discloses, "There was a lot of interest from some big players in the beginning." Despite valiant attempts to present the brand's future profitability though, deal after potential deal fell through. Things quickly deteriorated from bad to desperate. Still, he hung on to his conviction that triumph lay in the hands of someone who sincerely believed in Cordings. Then the questioned dawned on him - who would make a better someone than Noll himself? "I had long conversations with my wife and after a great deal of deliberation, I decided to buy Cordings." But he was a bit short on the selling price and was given a week to either come up with the money or an alternate solution. Otherwise the shop was going to be shuttered for good.

Noll had one audacious idea left up his sleeve. With little left to lose, he pulled it out. He made what turned out to be a crucial telephone call to one of the shop's prominent customers and requested a meeting. Once the appointment was set, he sweated over his prepared speech. And not just because the shop's survival depended on it but because the person on whom he was counting to become an investor was more than a garden variety celebrity, he was a veritable living legend - Eric Clapton. Sure, Clapton came into the shop with some regularity and always conducted himself absent of ceremony. But that didn't make him any less *the* Eric Clapton. In a career spanning some fifty years, the famed singer, composer and guitar player is the only performer to have been inducted thrice into the Rock and Roll Hall of Fame as a member of the bands Yardbirds, then Cream, and as a solo performer. He was knighted CBE in 2004.

Noll relates, "I was told by his assistant that he could come by the shop at ten the following morning. But then I got another call at the last minute letting me know that all of Sir Eric's children had contracted the flu and he couldn't make it. This only added to the suspense. At last, he did show up a week later. I stood ready to give this 20-minute comprehensive presentation on our merits and how his investment would be worthwhile. And I was only a couple of minutes into it when he gestured for me to stop. I felt my heart sink and thought all was lost. Then, after what seemed like a long pause, he flat out said he would do it!" Noll says Sir Eric has been very vocal about his admiration for Cordings, "His first purchase here was a three-piece, moss green herringbone tweed suit. He said it was the most well-made suit he had ever worn. And soon, he was coming in to the shop almost every week. Sir Eric likes our famous Covert coat so much he got four of them, two in each color!" Noll adds that having been a loyal customer, Sir Eric has an invaluable perspective as a partner. Schedule permitting, he also helps select the tweeds and provides intelligent feedback as well as his own ideas on design directions.

Those designs are conceived out of a strict adherence to the house's aforementioned five core pieces, either as seasonal or updated variants. Altogether new products still emanate from the core and may be considered as organic ancillaries. "We try to cover everything from socks to hats and all points in between," says Noll. "We are often inspired by our archives. For example, the Livingstone Jacket was adapted from a house style from seventy years ago. Our Wayfarer jacket, on the other hand, is a hybrid of a tailored jacket and a field coat made from our Covert cloth. It features practical shoulder pleats and elbow patches but we've given it a modern touch with calf leather trim at the cuffs." The tweed trousers are equally beguiling with its traditional hallmarks like a high waist, button flies, deep front pleats, and eschewing belt loops for side adjusters and brace buttons. But, they look modern with the leaner cut down the legs.

"The collection always starts with cloth," says Noll. "We buy our tweeds from mills such as Lovat, Harris, Magee, Johnstons, Fox Brothers, these British and Irish mills that have been weaving tweed for centuries. They intrinsically understand how to make the perfect cloth because it is very much a part of who and what they are. Plus, their use of color and pattern is second to none. Like Cordings they have all been around for centuries and their expertise within the businesses is phenomenal." He does make a point of qualifying that they have also begun dealing with some mills in the continent, albeit with a caveat. "Instead of 'performance' cloths, what we try to do is to look at ways of using traditional, natural cloths and construction methods which have inherent 'technical' qualities. For example we have developed a cotton coat for AW2019 that uses tightly woven 100% cotton that is still virtually waterproof. And our tweed jackets are in fact inherently water resistant. Our ethos is very much that we make garments that are built to be worn for decades. So functionality is the key in everything we do. Any design details have to have a purpose and not to be there for show."

Since Noll took over as managing director, Cordings has once again flourished. It has even been able to open a new store in 2015 at the spa town of Harrogate, situated along the edge of Yorkshire Dales. Its internet presence has also been rewarding in terms of attracting customers who otherwise aren't able to come to the store in person. In acknowledgement of the importance of seeing to the brand's continual relevance in the internet age, it has instigated a 2020 website upgrade, offering new user-friendly features to enhance customer experience. "We've gained a strong online business, half of which originate overseas, specifically from North America and Europe. Of course, we're popular in major cities like Paris or New York but we do ship to small towns and villages globally." He adds, "And though it constitutes a smaller part of our market, our ladieswear range is thriving." When asked what these ostensibly disparate people might have in common, he replies, "I think what binds our customers together is an appreciation for the tradition attached to owning a Cordings item along with the assurance that they are made with the utmost quality." Music legends are handy in a pinch, but at Cordings, the garments are what truly sing.

- - - - - - - -

Levity aside, creative and financial mismanagement aren't the only possible culprits for the failure of a business. How many small tailoring concerns, no matter how prestigious, must have withered away in the wake of time's mere passage? Back when an individual's station in life was inextricably linked to the family's trade and craft, apprenticeship and eventual work in the same arena was all but assured, especially if one didn't have the wherewithal to do anything else. And even when mores progressed to permit independent ambitions, familial obligation could still have been unavoidable. For those reasons, family-owned establishments are very often inevitably willed to one's progeny. At the oldest bespoke tailor in Scotland, Stewart Christie & Co, however, four generations of the Lowe family that had owned and operated the company had come to an abrupt halt. The last man standing was Duncan Lowe, who had no children to whom the business could be entrusted, and was therefore faced with the quandary of what to do when there is no heir.

The origin of Stewart Christie & Co. traces back to the founding of woolen drapers and hatters Marshall & Aitken in the 1700s. A couple of centuries later, in 1933, two other tailoring concerns - Messrs. Christie and Sons and J. Stewart and Sons (both founded in the early 1800s) — were amalgamated with Marshall & Aitken into Stewart Christie & Co. While the contribution of Marshall & Aitken's archives that date all the way to 1720 cannot be overstated, the names of the latter shops took precedence because both held royal warrants from King George V. Today, Stewart Christie is still qualified for those warrants and is responsible for producing replacement uniforms and tending to everything from the linings to the trimmings in the garments of the royal guards.

Lowe was still in his twenties when he was in effect conscripted into the business by his father (also called Duncan). His heart was set on becoming a gentleman farmer. But his sense of duty prevailed and he took over Stewart Christie & Co, no matter how begrudgingly. He eventually did arrive at a compromise by splitting his schedule between farming and tailoring. But after over forty years of labor, he was ready to hang up his shears. Left with no one to whom the business could be passed, Lowe was determined only to sell to people who would honor his family's legacy.

And clearly not one to shirk on his duties, Lowe patiently did his due diligence on any interested parties. In 2015, he found the right buyers in Victoria "Vixy" Rae and Daniel Fearn, whose work at the tweed garments brand Walker Slater (Est 1989) was an excellent demonstration of their esteem for and experience in well-made clothing. Vixy was all too aware of the burden of responsibility she would be undertaking before she and business partner Daniel dared assume their self-appointed roles as "custodians" to Stewart Christie & Co.

"Daniel and I have been great friends for twenty years and share the same work ethic and vision," says Vixy. "I'm very old school and Daniel and I were both already unhappy with the industry moving toward overseas sourcing. We heard about the possibility of Stewart

Christie closing and were disheartened by it. We thought we could work together to prevent that while helping preserve the traditions of the craft." The respect, and perhaps a little bit of awe, Vixy held for the establishment is rooted in remembering how she walked past this Stewart Christie & Co shop, still in the same Georgian building, every day as a child growing up in Edinburgh. Daniel reiterates they weren't looking to re-invent the brand but to underscore everything that made Stewart Christie extraordinary.

To ease the transition, they retained the existing staff, notably head cutter and tailor Terence McClelland, who's been with the shop for over twenty years. The more difficult task Vixy and Daniel faced was updating operations and bringing Stewart Christie into the 21st century. Record keeping and invoicing were all still being done on paper using a typewriter. There was no website, official logo, or label. Some refurbishing was also called for, the most conspicuous of which ended up being the shop's now hunter green facade with taller windows that let in an abundance of natural light. Subtle cosmetic changes were also undertaken within the work spaces. True to their goal Vixy and Daniel made certain these were not jarringly dramatic renovations. They replaced veneer display shelves with real mahogany and repurposed existing furnishings to surreptitiously transform the interiors into something befitting a classic bespoke tailor, country outfitter, and supplier of sporting clothes and highland wear.

Both Vixy and Daniel acknowledge how another crucial factor had also undergone a subtle change and that was the cloth. "Tweed has developed and become quite refined, so its use is now not only for the country but for city workers and everyday use too. But genuine tweed is still hard to find on the high street without discrepancies made somewhere in the make of a garment." Vixy says they have kept to their word of staying local with sourcing, "We work closely with Donald John McKay, the master weaver on the Isle of Harris who creates incredible Harris Tweed. There's also Rebecca Hutton, trained by Donald John, and also a wonderful weaver. Both are unique characters who dedicate themselves fully to the creation of these unique fabrics. We enjoy taking trips to visit them both and we take an empty van with us so that we can bring back as much fabric as we can!" They also source from Lovat Mill, Andrew Elliot, Lochcarron, Carloway, Harris Tweed Hebrides, Barrington, Moons, and Magee1866.

Another important update for the brand was the recent introduction of a ladies line, which Vixy personally designs. For the first collection, she says she didn't have to stray far from what works. "I was inspired by simple, genuine British designs and from our own archives. They provide a rich reference and we already look to them for menswear patterns from the last 150 years. We're also very much generation-led, not seasons-led, which means that even our designs for young professionals still hark back to the classics. Another great thing about being a bespoke tailor is that the customer designs for themselves and their own needs." She continues, "With the ladies collection of skirts, coats and jackets, I came up with 90% tweed and about 10% tartans and we've gotten a great reaction from models, judges, business ladies, everyone from ages 18 to 85." She says, so far the demand in both men's and ladies wear have been equally strong.

For all their positive growth, Vixy and Daniel are pleased keeping the business at a manageable scale. "We already work on estate tweeds for gamekeepers, ceremonial wear from judges' gowns to uniforms for the Royal Company of Archers and the Sovereign's bodyguards in Scotland. And we have a queue for bespoke and made-to-measure as it is! So wholesale and off-the-peg collections are not a priority for us. With that in mind, we are working on a global brand and do have an online shop. Still we aren't able to sell our stock to anyone else as we have only a few tailors on our premises. The in-store merchandise is supplemented by some of the foremost suppliers of knitwear, footwear, men's accessories, blankets and hats and other brands that are made only in the UK and Scotland."

But vital to the business is still the menswear: a range of three-piece ready-to-wear suits (from around £500 to £650), the growing made-to-measure services, and of course, bespoke. Most bespoke customers come from the US, Switzerland, Germany and London, many of whom are drawn to Stewart Christie's Savile Row caliber but at considerably lower prices. Of some concern, however, to both Daniel and Vixy, and indeed to the entire industry, is replenishing the talent pool with future tailors. In 2012, Daniel was elected the youngest member of the Edinburgh Incorporation of Tailors, a trade body that's been in existence for over six centuries. Vixy, on the other hand, made history by becoming its first-ever female member. Vixy admits to having been initially terrified "sitting round a table with 12 older characters." But she chuckles, "They needed some energy, I think." She remarks though that this is indicative of the need to attract promising talents to come up the ranks. "People do come out of college as designers but not enough on the technical side," she says. Daniel adds that there are also those who leave school without knowing what to do. He says that all the good of the recovering demand for tweed would be for naught if the people with the skills to make them continue to dwindle. He insists that more should be done to get people into the crafts. One solution, he says, is the creation of the Scottish Vocational Qualification (SVQ) for bespoke cutting and tailoring, not just to set standards but to instill pride in the mastering of these skills.

Through Stewart Christie & Co and the Incorporation of Edinburgh Tailors, Daniel and Vixy worked with schools and other companies including Edinburgh College, Glasgow Clyde College, Heriot Watt University, Creative Scotland, Savile Row Bespoke, Johnstons of Elgin, Alex Begg, and Deryck Walker to create the qualifying requisites. Together, they designed the SVQ based on the National Occupational Standards for Bespoke Cutting & Tailoring and other mandatory specifics to artisanal hand craft skills and knowledge in tailoring, production, and cutting practices. Daniel says he would love to set up local apprenticeship programs similar to those in Savile Row, "I feel there is so much skill in Scotland, both male and female, and we need to grab on to that," he says. Vixy thinks it may be beneficial as well to someday set up a tailoring school. She says, "We're losing so much craft and skills and it would be great to get young people back into it to ensure these traditions we hold so dear will still be there tomorrow."

VIII

Love Could Really Be Like a Broadway Show

Bewilderment clouded the faces of the people at Alan Flusser when they opened the package they had received from London. They held up the Dashing Tweeds cloth and couldn't quite understand what they were seeing. On check patterned cloth, the longer side of the rectangle is almost always woven to run along the length of the fabric in order to produce a generally desirable elongating effect in a completed garment. "But the dominant side of the check on the Dashing Explorer fabric we received was horizontal, as were the reflective 3M fibers," says Andrew. After quick deliberation, their apprehension was assuaged by noting how Will's slim and tall stature could not only make the fabric work but give the suit something extra. "The horizontal lines on someone with an already broad body shape might have appeared unflattering," Andrew points out. "On Will, however, we reached an assent that it could instead lend an air of boldness and eccentricity."

It was also then decided to make a minor revision to the original plan of making a four-piece suit - jacket, waistcoat, trousers, and plusfours. An offshoot of the baggy-kneed knickerbocker, plus-fours were commonly worn in the 1920s for golf or cycling. The number following the word "plus" in plus twos, plus fours, plus eights, etc., refers to the inches the garment extends below the knee. Will had hoped to have one included so he could have both a basic suit and a cycling ensemble. But Andrew had been reading an estate catalog of the Duke and Duchess of Windsor when he happened to notice a photo of the Prince of Wales wearing knickerbockers. The caption contained a description that prompted an ingenious idea.

Andrew says, "Apparently, the Prince disliked the constricting knee buckles that usually secured each leg on such garments. So he had his plus-fours constructed in a way that its bloused woolen cloth buttoned internally to the cotton lining. We thought we could apply the same logic by constructing full trousers with legs that could be folded inside themselves and thereby be easily convertible into plus-fours. We just needed to have a special tab on the inside of the cuffs to hide buttons on the interior seams." Fortunately, the wide and deeply pleated trousers that Will wanted anyway made this possible to accomplish sans unsightly aberrations. The material and the pattern with the important notes on how the suit was to be constructed were thus sent off to their made-to-measure factory.

The tricky part for the Alan Flusser team, of course, was to make sure the entire suit would still appear contemporary. With the aforementioned plus-four trousers, this was already going to be a substantially retro-styled garment. Any more precious and it could very easily be relegated into the realms of fetishization, caricature, or costume. And had Will been willing to don a suit that could be perceived as a costume, which he wasn't, even costumes are expected to adhere to their proper time and setting.

- - - - - - - -

Enter stage right: actor Benjamin Walker as Chris Keller. He appeared in a brown, windowpane tweed jacket in the 2019 revival of Arthur Miller's post WWII play "All My Sons". Under the direction of Jack O'Brien for the Roundabout Theatre Company, the play is set in an unnamed American town in the Midwest, and examines the lives of a family ensnared in a corporate conspiracy and divided loyalties. For this production, costume designer Jane Greenwood was responsible for outfitting Walker and the rest of the stellar cast, which included film actress Annette Bening. Originally from Liverpool, Jane was inducted into the American Theater Hall of Fame in 2003 and received a Tony award for lifetime achievement in the theater in 2014. This multi-nominated and awarded costume designer's body of work is of such scope they include everything from the 1983 network miniseries "Kennedy" and the 1980 disco-tastic cult favorite "Can't Stop the Music" (with Theoni V. Aldredge contributing to the all-white "Milkshake" number) to the original 1994 staging of Stephen Sondheim's "Passion" and the 2016 stage revival of Lillian Hellman's "Little Foxes". Jane has also served as professor of design at the Yale School of Drama since 1976.

The jacket Jane created to be worn by Walker for the Miller play is merely one of innumerable details viewers and audiences often take for granted in the approximations of places and historic settings crucial for the suspension of disbelief in films, television or onstage. For the talented people working backstage, the main goal (at least often enough) is to bring the public into a world that appears authentic to its environs. Jane's designs were attached to the original period of the play, showing what young people wore after the second world war. But for a play set in Wherever, USA, the proceedings here were also meant to convey timelessness. By inference, the story could be transpiring at this very minute and the jacket would still make perfect sense. It was the character's relative youth that informed the styling. "I thought a nice tweed sport coat paired with trousers (as opposed to a complete suit) was the appropriate look for the age of Ben's character," she explains. "We started with an actual vintage tweed jacket as a reference point and tried to replicate it as closely as possible." Jane felt that tweed would impart the right verisimilitude to the character as well as the scene.

But depending on the nature of a show on film, television or stage, costumes are often subject to multiple criteria beyond being simply appropriate for a character or setting. Between performances, for example, to facilitate quick changes without losing valuable seconds fiddling with buttons, some costumes have to be equipped with snaps, velcro, or hidden zippers. Others are made explicitly for extensive movement across the stage or set, especially for dancers or the chorus. During her brief stint designing for MGM motion pictures, Chanel is reported to have created three versions of the same costume for an actress. One was specifically crafted for fluid motion during a dance sequence; yet another to appear at its most flattering while standing; and one more best worn while seated. Shows with fantastical stories to tell may need additional wire riggings worked underneath parts of the garment, enabling the performer to take flight or do what production people call "wire work" stunts. So a costume is not necessarily as it appears exactly onstage, but a very important part of maintaining an illusion, for drawing the audience past the footlights and into the unfolding story on the boards.

To accomplish her production-mandated objectives, Jane has to be a stickler for costumes that look as genuine as possible. "Most modern fabrics are treated to have a soft drape," she says. "And if I am working on a period show, those would simply not work. To find just the right cloth that can be used to create vintage costumes is not easy." Fortunately, there are tweeds. Still, because of several other factors from stage lighting and an actor's complexion to the character's socio economic status, the right pattern to use can be an issue. "We were lucky to find this English manufacturer who had a selection of wonderful fabrics and once we saw this windowpane tweed, we knew straight away it was perfect," says Jane. "It wasn't too thick but it had a nice crisp hand." And the pattern was pronounced enough to be visible from the nosebleed section.

Interestingly, Jane had already attempted to use tweed on two previous productions, neither of which worked out particularly well. In the 1978 staging of the William Douglas-Home (1912-1992) comedy "Kingfisher" by director Lindsay Anderson (1923-1994), legendary actor Sir Rex Harrison (1908-1990) played Sir Cecil Warburton, a novelist trying to win back an old love played by Claudette Colbert (1903-1996). During preparations for the production at the Biltmore (now the Samuel J Friedman Theater), Sir Rex somehow got it into his head that he should wear a tweed suit for one of the scenes. Jane acquiesced after reaching the conclusion that yes, it was character appropriate. So they went ahead and had one made by Sir Rex's own Savile Row tailor. Alas, during dress rehearsals, the tweed suit became too unbearably hot to wear beneath the intense Klieg lights. The esteemed actor was drenched in sweat and kept stopping scenes to take a breath. Jane recounts, "We tried repeatedly before we all threw up our hands in sheer exasperation. We had to replace the tweeds with lightweight wool, probably closer to 12/13 oz." She sighs, "But by doing so we had to resign ourselves to the fact that our new costume didn't have as strong a pattern or presence."

Then, in 2009, for a limited-run production of Samuel Beckett's (1906-1989) "Waiting for Godot" at (the current theater incarnation of) Studio 54, director Anthony Page wanted actor John Goodman to wear a tweed suit. Jane says, "Both Anthony and I fell in love with the pattern on this heavy tweed check, which looked so good onstage." They enlisted famed costume designer John David Ridge to manufacture the suit. But again, tweed proved problematic and caused Goodman to perspire profusely. The actor also complained that the weight of the suit would be too much for him to endure during the lengthier scenes. They had to go back to Ridge and asked him to recreate the suit in linen. Having learned her lesson, for "All My Sons", Jane left Walker's jacket unlined. She says, "Since he only wears the jacket for the one scene, it was easier to convince him to wear tweed." And that proved to be the proverbial charm of the third try. But that Jane would consider attempting to use tweed again for one of her shows is a testament to the cloth's virtue as a signifier of socio cultural, intellectual, and economic status.

- - - - - - - -

John David Ridge's own history with employing tweeds for the theater goes all the way back to 1976. He was then an assistant to Sir Cecil Beaton and they were reproducing the original costumes of the 1956 production of "My Fair Lady" for the twentieth anniversary revival directed by Jerry Adler at the St. James Theatre. Ian Richardson

(1934-2007) was stepping into the role of cantankerous professor Henry Higgins, a character that has inadvertently contributed much to cementing (especially in the minds of Americans) the myopic association of tweeds to intellectual gentlemen of a certain age (and dour dispositions).

John's career in costume and design has been staggeringly prolific and protean. He was costume department head at the Juilliard School from 1970 to 1973 and design director at Halston in 1989. His theater work has ranged from supervising costumes of gothic splendor (derived from designs by Edward Gorey, 1925-2000) for Dennis Rosa's 1977 staging of "Dracula" at the Martin Beck Theatre, and serving as associate designer with John Bury for the Peter Shaffer play and Peter Hall directed "Amadeus" at the Broadhurst Theatre in 1980, to creating Tony-nominated original designs for the 1999 revival of Christopher Fry's (1907-2005) comedy "Ring Round the Moon" (an adaptation of Jean Anouilh's "Invitation to the Castle") starring Toby Stephens at the Lincoln Center Theatre. His cinematic output is equally impressive since he was, for a few years, making costumes for a multitude of Hollywood productions. He's responsible for Jeff Bridges' period tweed suits, from the Academy Award-winning designs of Judianna Makovsky (who was once an assistant to Jane Greenwood), in Gary Ross' 2003 horse racing drama "Seabiscuit". He also produced Chanel-like tweed ensembles for Faye Dunaway in her role as a ruthless Manhattan hotel mogul in the 1996 Ken Kawpis comedy "Dunston Checks In".

For all those glitzy Hollywood projects, however, John admits his heart has always belonged to the theater. He makes regular trips to the University of Florida School of Theater and Dance to teach a masterclass on costume design. By and large though, John has become selective of the kind of work he accepts these days. He recently completed costumes for the Apple+ TV series "Dickinson" slated to stream in 2020. He divulges, "I purposely moved away from the dizzying madness of Hollywood and New York for some peace and quiet, but am willing to work on the right projects." And the one he simply couldn't dismiss was the call from Opera Australia in 2015 asking if was willing to make the same costumes from that 1956 debut production of "My Fair Lady" for a sixtieth anniversary revival in Sydney, under the direction of none other than the original Eliza Doolittle herself, Dame Julie Andrews. Of course, John wasn't there when the Alan Jay Lerner (1918-1986) and Frederick Loewe (1901-1988) musical opened at the Mark Hellinger Theatre. But as mentioned, he was for the 1976 revival, and once more (as associate costume designer with Sir Cecil) for the 1981 iteration, which marked the much-heralded return of Rex Harrison to the role of Professor Higgins at the Uris Theatre (rechristened the Gershwin Theatre in 1983).

John was thrilled by the invitation but maintained a reservedly optimistic attitude. Although Opera Australia had previously produced well-received stagings of Richard Rodgers (1902-1979) and Oscar Hammerstein II's (1895-1960) "South Pacific" and "The King and I" in 2012 and 2014 respectively, he wanted to be sure this treatment of "My Fair Lady" would be nothing less than a world class tribute to what Sir Cecil had accomplished all those years ago. Whatever he may have been expecting, John was still unprepared for the assault of memories and emotions he experienced at the first table read. "I teared up," John confesses. "They don't do shows like this anymore!"

But the task itself was not at all going to be easy. He found very few photographic records of either the 1956 or the 1976 productions. And because the designs had been emphatically revised for the 1964 film version (starring Harrison and Audrey Hepburn), he could hardly refer to that. It is said that only the costumes of the black-and-white Ascot scene had remained mostly intact in all the productions and that they were inspired by the couture creations of Paul Poiret (1879-1944). "Cecil's knowledge of fashion was encyclopedic," John says. "He based that black and white scene from the 1910 Black Ascot held right after the death of King Edward VII when, as a sign of mourning, everyone came in their finest black and white outfits. But because Cecil was aware that mauve was also a color of mourning he made Julie's costume for the Broadway version in that hue, giving dramatic license for her to stand out while staying true to the concept he had in mind."

Thus John had to judiciously scour through his sketchbooks from decades ago to reconstitute what he could, as faithfully as he could. He spent over a year shuttling to and from Sydney, working on the production and traveling the globe in search of skilled crafts people who could still execute the intricate hand embroidery and embellishments he needed. "I found a hand embroiderer in LA and supervised the work via Skype. And, because of the time difference, this was often done at two in the morning!" He sighs, "But this is a dying art. Very soon, you wouldn't be able to find people with the kind of skills necessary to craft these kinds of pieces, and make them well." He sourced some fabrics from Germany and found his tweed in the UK. He recounts, "I had a swatch of the original tweed with me on a shopping trip to London. The material was a brownish taupe and thought maybe if I looked around the fine fabric stores, I might find something close enough to it. I took a chance and showed it to the good people at Holland & Sherry. I asked if they had something similar in stock. To my surprise, they offered to recreate it!" Out of the tweeds Holland & Sherry made, John produced two three-piece suits (one each for the first and second acts) for the British actor Alex Jennings, who would play Professor Higgins.

Before the musical opened, Opera Australia producer John Frost crowed to members of the press that the costumes were going to be exact replicas, "down to the last sequin". The revival was a smash, breaking the company's box office records of any previous performance. The show eventually toured to Melbourne and Brisbane. And John couldn't have been more pleased, thinking out loud that Sir Cecil would have been too. He concludes, "It was a wonderful experience. Working on those costumes was a joy and those for Professor Higgins could only have been made with tweed. Tweed is such an amazing fabric of genuine character that works so well on stage because it can suggest an era while staying eternally just beyond time itself."

Tracy Christensen, another multi award-winning costume designer, also uses the cloth to sway audience perceptions. "I have used tweed often for various characters and shows because it's practically a wonder fabric for conveying a wealth of strong connotations that precludes ponderous exposition," she says. "Depending on what story I'm trying to tell about someone in a play or a musical, tweed proves very handy in giving additional information to the viewers that may not be in the script. In a clear and unmistakable way, tweed can communicate in shorthand something about profession, attitude, economic standing, culture, season, values, functions, beliefs."

Born and raised in the rural outskirts of Racine, WI, Tracy was always artistic but came upon her actual calling when she went to grad school at Mason Gross School of the Arts at Rutgers University (Est 1776). She recounts, "In the fall of my first year, a colleague of one of my professors there called her up looking for a couple of students to come to New York and hand sew some latex 'mud' onto the bottoms of costumes for a show. I immediately volunteered with a friend and we high-tailed it to the Barbara Matera Ltd costume shop in lower Manhattan where we sat for three days stitching (fake) mud and taking in all the thrill of working on Broadway!" The show was the original production of Stephen Sondheim's fairy tale opus "Into the Woods", which had its out-of-town tryouts at San Diego's Old Globe Theater in 1986 before taking a bow on Broadway at the Martin Beck (now the Al Hirschfeld) theatre a year later. Tracy says, "I was so fortunate to meet the show's designer Ann Hould-Ward. I was then luckier to reconnect with her after I graduated. She became my mentor and we worked together for a few years before I became a full-fledged designer myself." Tracy would have her own stints in several other Sondheim shows, costuming the Lonny Price directed stage productions of The New York Philharmonic's "Company" with Neil Patrick Harris in 2011 and "Sweeney Todd: The Demon Barber of Fleet Street" in 2014 with Emma Thompson, Bryn Terfel, and Audra McDonald.

Yoked as it is to a set of ideas and ideals, tweed as storytelling device has figured prominently and effectively in some of Tracy's other works. In 2012, she brought it center stage in the costume for actress Audrie

Neenan who was playing a character called "Miss Tweed" in a revival of the musical whodunit parody "Something's Afoot". This production, jointly penned by James McDonald, David Vos, and Robert Gerlach, with additional music by Ed Linderman, was held at the same theater where it had originally premiered in 1973, the Goodspeed Opera House, in East Haddam, Connecticut. Tracy says, "The character was a broadly drawn version of Agatha Christie's Miss Marple. And with a name like Miss Tweed, it was clear what direction one needs to go with her costume fabrication. But more than that, we wanted her to be very British, very proper, businesslike, and display a seemingly rugged visual. I also needed a pattern with heightened tonality to underscore the comedy of the show. And all those things were achieved with tweed."

Based on intensive research into 1930s fashions, she came up with "A single breasted jacket in herringbone tweed with rounded notched lapel and exterior pockets on the lower front sides that closed with a flap. There was a self-belt with a rectangular plastic buckle at center front. The matching skirt had a slight bit of 30's shaping but also some pleats for ease in movement," she recounts. "This character is very pragmatic and of a certain age that made for specific choices around the length of the skirt (well below the knee) and in the conservative cut of the suit jacket. The color was a lovely mauve, pale burgundy tweed, moving away from the obvious tan or grey to something that worked in the realm of a broad musical comedy where brighter color supports the overall tone of the piece."

Four years after that, Tracy worked on Nina Raine's award-winning play "Tribes" directed by Jenn Thompson for the Barrington Stage Company in Berkshire County, Massachusetts. "The family depicted in the play is British and the father, Christopher (played by actor C. David Johnson) is an intelligent but complicated man - learned, harsh, hard-drinking, and someone slightly disheveled. The director and I immediately thought of translating those ideas via tweed jackets that had aged, distressed, and well-worn qualities." Later that same year, Tracy was called on to design for Tennessee Williams' (1911-1983) "The Glass Menagerie" at the University of Utah. For the characters of siblings Tom and Laura Wingfield (played by Zachary Prince and Hanley Smith respectively), Tracy wanted to express the haughty characteristics of a genteel Southern family that may have fallen close to destitution but had stayed tenaciously ungovernable. "We went with creating new garments using a good, dense brown wool tweed, which was very important in getting the right look of the period suits of the 1930s for the Tom Wingfield character. He is someone in turmoil on many levels of his life and very much does not care about his appearance. He sleeps in this suit and has no stake in presenting himself to the world with any polish."

For his sister Laura Wingfield, a retiring young woman who's been infantilized by her mother, Tracy designed practical wool skirts. Tracy explains, "There is nothing fashion forward about Laura - she is simply trapped in a situation that inhibits her from crossing a certain set of parameters. I found a lovely softer wool tweed that I made up into a beautiful A-line skirt, in a burgundy and tan check that had a lot of interest and energy. The shape was gently fitted through the waist and hips, then releasing into a series of pleats that gave the actress complete freedom of movement, allowing her to easily sit on the floor and manage her character's leg disability with no problem. The hem was relatively low for the period and the cut conservative, but this demonstrated the character's modesty and innocence.

"Scotland and England have fantastic wools obviously but I always start in New York," Tracy says regarding how she sources her fabrics. "We have a diverse and expansive fabric selection here in the city. I found the novelty color and the scale of weave I wanted for the suit of 'Miss Tweed' here; although I did source wools for other characters in that show from Holland & Sherry for authentic British looks." Once she has her fabrics, Tracy will often have them manufactured at several costume shops with which she's dealt before. "There are many in New York (and other cities) which specialize in costumes for Broadway, Off Broadway, and everything in between." According to her, "Most regional theaters do have in-house costume shops with drapers and tailors. And I've worked on shows using a couple of wonderful out-of-town tailors who are based in Baltimore and Chicago. But it's much preferable to work with people local to where the show is happening so they are readily available for fittings or those unavoidable last minute alterations.

"Budget is, of course, a major factor in figuring out what is or isn't possible for any show." Best case scenario, costumes are designed and custom made, but other options include purchasing or renting something ready-made. For main characters, usually only one of each costume is required. But there are shows when a costume has to be duplicated for aforementioned stunts such as simulating flight or acrobatic feats. She adds, "On Broadway, for those with extended runs, a new one may have to be produced for a new actor taking over the role. We also do make the same costume for the understudy who may wear a different size. In smaller theaters though, that may not be affordable and some compromise has to be reached. But if I had the option and funds, it's great to be able to make the best choices for character and story rather than going with something because it's economical.

"Costuming is an integral part of telling a story for the theater," says Tracy. And she points out how there's more to tweed than the suggestion of a period story. "Tweed can speak volumes beyond character and what they are doing in a particular scene. It is, plainly put, timeless," she insists. "A costume designer just has to be conscious of how to use it. A tweed jacket from the 1960s is not the same as one from 1920 or from 2018. It's very versatile and can be manipulated in ways to set a specific tone without losing the integrity tweeds bring to the table."

– – – – – – – –

On film, tweed has appeared in major Hollywood productions far too numerous to list. Of course, there are stand outs. In the 1973 Ted Post directed sequel "Magnum Force", Clint Eastwood returned as maverick police officer "Dirty" Harry Callahan wearing a single breasted herringbone tweed sportcoat with flapped pockets, horizontal front yokes, and single pointed back yoke. But as action heroes go, no one but no one out-debonairs James Bond. Almost all the Bonds at one point or another, have worn tweeds: George Lazenby in Peter R. Hunt's 1969 "On Her Majesty's Secret Service", Roger Moore in Lewis Gilbert's 1979 "Moonraker" and in John Glen's 1985 "A View to a Kill", and Pierce Brosnan in Michael Apted's 1999 "The World Is Not Enough". In the franchise's 1964 installment "Goldfinger" directed by Guy Hamilton, the first James Bond, Sean Connery wore a traditional barleycorn pattern hacking jacket with slanted front pockets and a ticket pocket on the right. Fashion historians have noted however that the details of the jacket, like its narrower lapels and horn buttons, were still very 1960s. It also bears mentioning that Sir Sean donned tweeds, a full three-piece suit, in yet another iconic role as Henry Jones Sr., the father of Harrison Ford's swashbuckling hero in Steven Speilberg's 1989 adventure picture "Indiana Jones and the Last Crusade." Ford wears his own three-piece tweed suit as well during scenes in which his character teaches antiquities at the fictional Marshall College.

However, there are probably as many controversies in the use or absence of tweeds in entertainment. An egregious creative choice that did not escape eagle-eyed fashion observers was the climactic scene of director Sam Mendes' 2012 picture "Skyfall". As Daniel Craig's James Bond battled the bad guys at his ancestral Scottish Highlands estate Skyfall, instead of being in tweed, he was in a Tokihito Yoshida-designed olive neo-Barbour jacket. And as if to salt the wounded purists, it had buttons instead of the traditional zipper. If it's any consolation, in director Rian Johnson's 2019 crowd-pleaser "Knives Out", Craig gets to wear a Bond-worthy custom tweed suit and topcoat, courtesy of costume designer Jenny Eagan. Set against a wintry Massachusetts landscape, the picture has Craig playing a heavily-accented Southern sleuth who arrives at a rather ominous country house to investigate the sudden and puzzling death of a wealthy novelist played by the one-and-only Christopher Plummer. Sure, it was Chris Evans' cream sweater that got all the press, but it was no accident that it was Craig's tweed suit that was mentioned in a line during the movie.

Though Johnson's picture was a refreshingly modern take on the classic murder mystery, this entertainment genre is no less beloved for all its built-in tropes. A couple of years ago, director Kenneth Branagh came out with the umpteenth version of Agatha Christie's (1890-1976) "Murder on the Orient Express". As in previous iterations, this was another all-star cast led in this go around by the ever dazzling Michele Pfeiffer, Dame Judi Dench, and Branagh himself delivering an action hero take on the fastidious detective Hercule Poirot. No matter the production, or era-dictated tweaks, the preferred (and admittedly perfect) mise-en-scène for this story is the year in which the book was first published, 1934. And because it is a mystery after all, the characters are often depicted as ciphers instead of "real" people. Thus, a period-set story on a luxury train with charismatic actors portraying archetypes becomes the perfect opportunity to pull out the tweeds. Additionally, since this big budget picture was shot in 70mm high resolution film, every detail that could possibly show up on screen was meticulously designed. And costume designer Alexandra Byrne did not disappoint.

For the denouement, Branagh framed his actors behind a long table, like Leonardo da Vinci's "The Last Supper" with Pfeiffer as a self-sacrificing Christ figure at the center. She is flanked on both sides by the other suspects huddled together in tweed suits and topcoats, most distinctly Willem Dafoe, Leslie Odom Jr., Sergei Polunin, Josh Gad, and Manuel Garcia-Rulfo, along with Tom Bateman standing to the side. This scene calls attention to how professional costume designers are accustomed to factoring in the sets. Here, Byrne uses the tweeds in vivid and warm contrast to the chilly white backdrop of ice and snow. During the round of press for the film, Bryne was widely quoted for having sourced 1930s designed fabrics and had some custom made in Scotland. She also went through vintage dealers, fairs, markets, and costume shops to find authentic items to use. Paying heed to the classes and economic means of these motley characters, all of whom are concealing secrets incidentally, Byrne created an array of wonderfully textured garments befitting every single one of them.

The exploits of the other Poirot, David Suchet's popular rendition of the Belgian crime solver, showed its fair share of tweeds throughout his ITV series run from 1989 to 2013. Since television sets became a fixture in households, a plenitude of tweeds have made appearances in hit shows throughout the years. Though there are instances in which its use is unavoidably straightforward in terms of a show's era and locale, it is in this format that tweed has effectively evaded stereotyping. To wit, for the first season of "Charlie's Angels" in 1976, costumer Ray Phelps dressed Farrah Fawcett's (1947-2009) bombshell of a private investigator Jill Munroe in a smartly cut Givenchy Sport tweed jacket.

Fast forward to Jonathan Nolan's near-future series, CBS' "Person of Interest" where New York becomes the battleground of two artificial intelligences and tweed is among the costumes. That show's style made a quantum leap when Academy Award-nominated costume designer Gary Jones came in during its third season (2013, staying on through its last in 2016) and he began outfitting actor Michael Emerson's billionaire-hacker Harold Finch in sumptuous tweed coats and suits for several episodes. Even for a show that had already made several in-universe inferences on the value of bespoke garments, Jones' contributions were immediately discernible. And they should. His IMDB credits include solo projects along with stylish and stylized collaborations with award winning-costume designer Anne Roth such as those for Brian de Palma's 1980 neo-slasher "Dressed to Kill", Mike Nichols' 1988 rags-to-corner office dramedy "Working Girl", and two classics from director Anthony Minghella (CBE, 1954-2008), "The English Patient" in 1996, and "The Talented Mr. Ripley" in 1999. That last picture was based on the 1955 Patricia Highsmith (1921-1995) novel of the same name, in which the titular Thomas Ripley murders and then takes on the persona of errant scion Dickie Greenleaf. In the book, Highsmith describes part of how Ripley went about to impersonate the well-shod Dickie: "He lay around all afternoon in his brown tweed suit". The motion picture is notable for using visual language in plumbing deeper still into the psychology of dress as identity, armor, status, costume, and disguise.

Tweed's versatility is also evident in its use for such diverse television and streaming shows, on both sides of the Atlantic, such as the Starz time travel romance "Outlander", HBO's noirish Prohibition era saga "Boardwalk Empire", and the USA Network modern day law firm drama "Suits". In "Peaky Blinders", the ongoing BBC Two series that premiered in 2013, a revolving door of costumers - from Stephanie Collie to Alison McCosh - have employed tweeds in creating a consistent yet still fictitious version of a real street gang from late 19th century Birmingham. A key feature is, of course, the eight paneled tweed caps from which the gang took its name, "Peaky Blinders". The three-piece tweed suits worn by actor Cillian Murphy, who plays lead character Thomas Shelby, were first custom tailored by Keith Watson. Though it is incumbent for the production people to ground the proceedings with a realistic tone, creative license was taken here and there. For instance, Murphy's herringbone tweed suits may be cut leaner around the chest and along the legs than they ought to be, but they're still quite period accurate with deeply pleated and high-waisted trousers. Lacking the budget to have everything custom made, however, other clothes and accessories are sourced from local suppliers including vintage shop Starry Starry Night in Glasgow, and Cosprop and Angels Costumes in London.

For another BBC show, "Sherlock", actor Benedict Cumberbatch played a present day version of the world's most famous detective. His Sherlock Holmes, garbed in very contemporary clothes, strikes an imposing figure in the tweed Milford coat by Belstaff for the show's pilot. And most recently, Netflix and the BBC co-produced a 2020 version of "Dracula" in which actor John Hefernan as Jonathan Harker walks unsuspectingly into the count's castle in a tweed traveling suit courtesy of costume designer Sarah Arthur. And on and on it goes, because as long as there are stories to be told, in one form or another, tweed will exist among the stars on screens great or small.

IX

⚜

A New Day for Those Good Old Dreams

Completion of Will's suit was near at hand. At the studio, Andrew recounts, "Meticulous planning went into the suit and the details we added with Alan's blessing. We put in lapels for the vest, side tabs, and a high fishtail back on the trousers so there wouldn't be any exposure of shirtwaist while cycling without a jacket." And to punctuate the sporty nature of this suit, they put in a half belt, patch pockets, and an action back - i.e. side gussets that would allow the arms unencumbered movement by the shoulder sleeves. Andrew says, "These bi-swing action backs are notoriously difficult to properly execute. They must open to provide a full range of motion, but close cleanly when the arm is at rest. A common solution tailors resort to is employing various types of elastic rigging between the blades. But that method would be unprepossessing on our quarter-lined coat." He adds, "Plus, there's the possibility they may snag. In the end, we needn't have worried. The bi-swing vents were tailored perfectly, neatly opening and closing on their own. We're pleased to now offer this and the suit's other custom-y details to our made-to-measure clients with full confidence in their quality." Although a made-to-measure suit ordinarily entails less work than a fully custom one, Andrew avers, "Throughout the fitting process, the differences experienced by our custom and made-to-measure clients are minimal."

Conventionally, a first fitting is held so the garment can be carefully inspected for how well it fits on a client's body. This is when everyone goes over the most infinitesimal of details. The trousers should break just so on the shoes. The jacket should hug, not squeeze, around the shoulders. Its sleeves must end a quarter to half an inch before the shirt sleeves. There should be no gap between the collars of the jacket and shirt. All these are surveyed so there are no unpleasant surprises at the end. Will showed up for the average two fitting sessions, which transpired with less issues than was anticipated. Andrew says, "It came down to some scooping out of the waistcoat fronts for a rakish 1930s flair, and a snugging of the high fishtail trousers into the small of the back." He adds, "The suit's twenty-three buttonholes were then each hand-sewn, including four on the converter tabs on the inside of the trouser cuffs, and four on each of the sleeves. We also gave the sleeves a deep 'turnback' of cloth so Will could fully unbutton them without exposing any lining."

Any requisite adjustment ought to be minor when dealing with a proper tailor or haberdasher. To avoid any misgivings it's important to engage someone who is able to completely understand what the client wants. Will was unquestionably in the hands of among the finest in the industry already. Furthermore, his needs were not so anomalous in a city where there is no shortage of shops that could've adequately met most of them. But, there is a multitude of other people whose needs may be construed as fairly more complicated. Fortunately, there are a number of tailors, brands, and small shops that have recently risen to the occasion. And it's the dawning of an overdue enlightened and egalitarian era in fashion that only underscores its power to affect the lives of so very many.

- - - - - - - -

An industrial warehouse in spitting distance of the Brooklyn Naval

Yard might not be the very first place to look for someone who can craft a fine bespoke suit. But, this is where Daniel Friedman and Rae Tutera provide the specialized services of Bindle & Keep. Inside, the studio is evocative of an old fashioned haberdashery with its brick walls and wood panelings. The suits on the racks may at first appear like those one finds in similar such establishments. Yes, they are bespoke and tagged with the names of the individuals for whom they were made. What truly distinguishes them though is how these are cut to the very specific needs of a heretofore ignored and indeed still marginalized but significantly growing market - the LGBTQ+ community. Here is where costume designer Eric Daman (who's worked on glamorous New York-based shows like the CW's "Gossip Girl") commissions suits for actor Asia Kate Dillon who plays the non-binary finance analyst Taylor Mason on the Showtime cable series "Billions".

As a point of clarification, the plus symbol trailing the generally used acronym LGBT(Q) covers nearly everyone on the spectrum, including Cisgender straight male and female allies. There are, to be sure, customers who are disinterested in the mission statement or the personal lives of the rest of the clientele, so long as Bindle & Keep produces well-made suits. Comprising the majority now, however, about 90% by Daniel's accounting, are those who may or may not necessarily be undergoing gender reassignment from female to male but are still considered outside preconceived and outdated norms. Of little doubt, many, if not all, have grappled with issues of gender conformity, body image, and sexuality in some form or another and at some point during their lifetimes. And they come from everywhere - obscure midwestern towns, other metropolitan areas, and from as distant countries as Mexico, Canada, Japan, and Australia.

When Daniel founded Bindle & Keep in 2011, he didn't have the slightest inkling how much a suiting business could transfigure lives, not to mention his very own. The circuitous route that brought him to that full realization may have begun when he was quite suddenly struck by a strange disorder, which rendered him incapable of reading or writing. On what had started out as an otherwise unremarkable night, Daniel was hard at work finishing a term paper. He already had a master's in architecture from the University of Pennsylvania and was only weeks away from another in real estate development at Columbia. He paused in the middle of a sentence when he noticed something odd. He couldn't seem to comprehend his own notes. "I felt like my eyes were sliding over the words. I couldn't lock onto them, like they were scrambling and moving all over the page," he relates. "My first thought was I may have had a stroke." What he hadn't considered right away was the possibility that it may have been a progression of a learning disability for which he had been diagnosed in his youth. Despite the veneer of academic accomplishments, Daniel had always struggled at school. Few were ever aware of how much effort he put into his studies and course applications. Throughout his school years, he fought for every single grade. When he was first trying to get into a good architecture program, rejection after rejection from universities where he applied never stopped him. Getting into one was as much about his love for design as it was to silence the lifelong inner voice that had ceaselessly berated him for being "stupid".

But this inability to read was something new and terrifying. After it subsequently set in that this disorder wasn't going to abate of its own volition, and that it was probably more serious than he first thought, Daniel went for a check-up. He had no reason to suspect he would then spend years consulting a cadre of specialists and neurologists, none of whom could offer so much as a verifiable prognosis, much less a certain course of treatment. While he lingered in a state of agonizing limbo, undergoing intermittent bouts of debilitating headaches, photosensitivity, and fatigue, the bills for doctors' appointments accumulated. He soon found himself marginally shy of abject penury and homelessness, forced into sleeping on friends' couches. But true to form, he wasn't about to let his mysterious impairment get the better of him. Daniel says, "I'm scrappy. I could still use my hands and I was willing to do whatever it took to survive." With the help of a friend called Allison Goldberg, he started a one-man interior design-slash-contractor business. "I did floor-to-ceiling remodeling, everything from fixtures to wiring to painting." And he was darned good at it. He parlayed the earnings from that into setting up Bindle & Keep.

"It wasn't a career trajectory I could have imagined. But on some basic level, there was something about men's suits that always interested me. I had a custom suit my parents got for me and it always made me feel more confident than I really did. I figured I could start a suiting business since it didn't require my being able to read or write." Although the absolute cause for his malady was never quite determined, medications were able to keep the severe symptoms at bay. With renewed purpose, Daniel made haste in getting his venture off the ground. "I conducted the first phase of the work in New York and found this factory in Thailand to make the suits for me. Any necessary alterations were done by this amazing seamstress I recruited, Dorota Wiencko (who remains a much valued part of the team today)." He recounts those early years, "I didn't have a place back then, so I went to my customer's homes or offices to measure them for a suit as if it was part of the personalized services I was offering." In truth, he operated out of a 1986 Toyota pickup, always parking at a discreet distance so none would be the wiser. The vehicle also happened to be his storage space. So he frantically drove all over town to deliver the suits as soon as possible because it would have been way too easy for any penny-ante thief to steal them from his pickup.

Concurrent to Daniel rebuilding his life, Rae Tutera was working as an archivist for various libraries and cultural institutions while blogging about trans life under the moniker "The Handsome Butch". Like an untold number of others who've grown up dealing with a cognitive dissonance between their birth sex and identity, Rae hand waved most of it away under cloaks of oversized Knicks jerseys and baggy flannel shirts. Many have no reason to go beyond the superficial idea that fashion is persona writ large. Yet the how and why of dressing is governed by cultural, social, economic, and personal complexities. For instance, fashion postulates that one dresses either to conform to one's tribe or in aspiration of belonging to another. So where was one to turn if fashion had not (yet) bothered to supply dressing for those who don't adhere to the only two stringently accepted gender classifications?

Although the closest thing to an outer expression of Rae's inner self has always been wearing menswear, nothing ever looked or felt quite right. And eventually, there came a day when the whole "tomboy" guise was clearly not cutting it anymore. Anything involving getting dressed for a social occasion or shopping for clothes inevitably ended in misery. And whatever Rae put on, the result was always the same: the contradictory yet simultaneous sensation of being unseen yet glaringly out of place. And somehow this was commonly accompanied by some nebulous yet nagging sense that everyone else around seemed to be carrying themselves with enviable aplomb, a misperception that only enflamed the discomfort in one's skin.

Consequently, Rae resolved to remedy this untenable situation by having a suit custom made by a tailor. In anticipation of ridicule or contempt, it took every ounce of courage to go to one. Once there, it became clear Rae's apprehension wasn't wholly unfounded. As sympathetic as the tailor tried to be, he still kept compulsively proportioning his pattern according to that of women's pantsuits, such as having a shorter jacket which flares at the hem. In hesitant stammers, Rae corrected him, explaining that it was to be a man's suit. "I barely managed the composure to simply stand there and ask for what I wanted. I couldn't bring myself to tell him I was planning on having top surgery. So I kept asking for the chest area to be minimized. And I didn't yet know how to put across the idea of a gender neutral suit." Still, the tailor complied as closely as he could with the directions he was given. And ultimately, Rae found the ordeal to have been worth it.

When the gray wool suit was ready to be tried on, it was an utter revelation. "I had been hiding inside my clothes for most of my life and putting that suit on and standing in front of a mirror was like meeting myself for the first time." Rae says "I wore it to a New Year's Eve party and I received so many compliments as if people were finally noticing me as well." The experience pulled Rae into the world of men's suiting. "I suddenly wanted to learn all about the business so I emailed a couple of companies including Bindle & Keep." After several emails to different brands, it was Daniel who responded. He says jokingly, "It was partly what was in the email but also because it was already the third one I received from Rae." He agreed to meet for a beer where Rae laid out the pitch for addressing the needs of a largely overlooked and often misunderstood population. And in Daniel's own words, the two of them "simply clicked".

Still, Daniel, who happens to be a straight, Jewish guy, knew next to nothing about the LGBTQ+ community. But he was receptive and willing to learn. And he admits there was much to learn. The 2011 landmark legalization of same sex marriages in Maine had already made available online a spate of wedding pictures for the two to study, mostly as a primer on what not to do. "A lot of those tuxedos were ridiculously too large," Rae says. Daniel elaborates, "Those who are born female would be around two inches narrower in shoulder span than those who were born male having the same body mass. So, something from the menswear department in their size would have shoulders that are already too broad. And that's just for starters because adding to the problem - the shoulder width of that jacket or shirt will have been constructed in proportion to the rib cage. Therefore, to get a garment that closes well over a female chest, many often buy a jacket or shirt in a larger size. And that's a mistake because now all the proportions are totally off."

With each client that showed up on their doorstep, Rae and Daniel became more adept at making suits addressing that problem - from gender neutral to outright masculine, depending on the requirements and preferences of the clients. Some of them may be in stages of transition. Others may have no such plans. "We have a straight male client who has always loved the suits we made for him so he had a Harris Tweed suit made for his wife," Daniel says. "And no, it was not a woman's suit. It was a gender neutral suit with a beautifully colored pattern, and cut precisely to her measurements." The tweeds Bindle & Keep uses come from the finest sources including Holland & Sherry, Abraham Moon, and Gladson. "Tweed is a wonderful cloth to work with," says Daniel. "It has weight and integrity and in many ways ideal for what we do. It doesn't crimp or cling to create unwanted curvatures. And once our clients realize there is no need for them to hide behind their clothes, they start being more daring in their color choices and willing to stand out." He declares, "If suits are supposed to be armor, tweed is like wearing a tank!"

Word about the brand slowly but surely circulated in the LGBTQ+ community, with "The Handsome Butch" blog its loudest advocate. And although Bindle and Keep started out as a "side hustle" for Rae, it became a full-time gig. Through community connections, Bindle & Keep got involved with the fashion and beauty queer media platform dapperQ and its annual runway shows. "We were there at the first one, which was held in a bar with very few people," says Rae. And they were there when it was later held at the Brooklyn Museum in front of hundreds including Rae's grandmother, who came in a wheelchair, bearing proud witness to the momentous occasion. Ten of the shop's clients volunteered to model their own Bindle & Keep suits for the show. Right on the heels of the customers came the media, ready to anoint the fledgling company the disruptor du jour. In the age when the industry was finally acknowledging the needs of diverse body shapes, sizes, and ethnicities, other gender fluid brands like Tomboy Tailors, Haute Butch, Saint Harridan, and Radimo were also cropping up. The limelight just happened to shine brighter on Bindle & Keep. When a story on the brand appeared in the New York Times in 2013, Daniel awoke to a deluge of emails from around the world, mostly laudatory and overflowing with gratitude, although perhaps to be expected, there was the usual smattering of hate messages.

To pick a nit however, most of the media coverage on Bindle & Keep often unwittingly reduce the situation by praising the idea that these garments were being made according to individual bodies, as though that wasn't what all bespoke tailors already do. In comparing ready-to-wear to Bindle & Keep, many writers end up simply focused on the advantages of bespoke. This isn't merely false analogy, it also misses the point. Nothing in the traditional craft of tailoring adequately prepares anyone on how to make a suit for a transgender person. To be fair, it often isn't about any deficiency in skill, it can also be a question of how a customer might be unable to clearly state what they want or whether the tailor is willing to listen.

Empathy, according to Daniel, is what makes Bindle & Keep unusual. Although he is also quick to add that anyone can provide that. Except, of course, few do. Here, these transgender or non-binary individuals find a safe space where they are able to tell their stories and made to feel that they can be who they truly are. Much weeping occurs at this studio (and Daniel's gigantic Bernese mountain dog Albert is always close by to provide comfort). First there's the catharsis of meeting Daniel and Rae, people who, at long last, were willing to hear them out and allay their trepidations. Of course, any reputable bespoke tailor knows enough to be a good listener. But theirs is not a vocation where it's an everyday occurrence to hear such personal and painful anecdotes. Bindle & Keep clients divulge heart-rending accounts of growing up in hostile environments, grappling with self-inflicted though largely unwarranted guilt or shame, having been relentlessly bullied most of their lives, subjected to violence, or shunned outright by their own families. And through it all, they are expected to suffer in quiet indignation.

They all arrive, in one way or another, cautiously vulnerable or openly wounded. And no matter how often their tales strike similar chords, hurt that's not supposed to show is always very acutely felt by Daniel and Rae. The two will then invariably and gently coax the client into revealing what they want in and from a bespoke suit. Somehow it almost never starts off with suits for grand, aggressive posturing. Many who come to the studio, too accustomed to seeing garments as convenient yet unwieldy covers, are hardly able to contemplate let alone verbalize what it is they are looking for or reasonably expect. They shield themselves from possible disappointment, afraid that they will yet again be betrayed, if not by the suit maybe by their own bodies. The next shedding of tears comes when they return to try on the finished suits. Those moments of a client in a suit standing before a mirror are of such poignancy and power that it never fails to astonish Daniel and

Rae how garments seem to confer validations of self. For the client, the act of slipping on a jacket becomes a potent, unapologetic act of claiming their true identities. Inevitably, the clients leave feeling their lives have somehow been irrevocably changed. Be that as it may, Daniel is all too aware the suits offer neither quick fix nor lasting cure. The hope is they might signify a new beginning for the people who place such trust in Bindle & Keep.

A new beginning was always going to be a leitmotif at Bindle & Keep. Its silhouette logo of a bindle-carrying gentleman (or non binary individual?) in a top hat, riding a penny farthing, already suggests as much. And the company has certainly already offered fresh starts for both Daniel and Rae, as it continues to do for the people who wear their suits. Daniel furthered that motivation in 2017 when once wrongfully incarcerated men, freed through the efforts of the Innocence Project, began receiving not only a new lease on life but bespoke suits courtesy of Bindle & Keep. A pro-bono organization founded in 1992 by Peter Neufeld and Barry Scheck, the Innocence Project evaluates countless cases in which a miscarriage of justice may have occurred. It then works to exonerate the innocent while promoting reforms in the judicial system. Without diminishing the torment of actual imprisonment, Daniel couldn't help but see parallels to the corporeal, mental, and emotional ones he, Rae, and their clients had all endured. And though suits, no matter how well made, may not be able to ameliorate trauma, Daniel reasons that they may conceivably imbue these men with the same sense of individuality, pride, and dignity felt by all Bindle & Keep customers.

Yet another kind of new beginning await those at Urban Outfitters' Athropologie in-store wedding brand BHLDN in its forthcoming collaboration with Bindle & Keep. For close to ten years, BHLDN has only ever sold bridal gowns, bridesmaid dresses, and wedding accessories to women. But soon, Bindle & Keep will be launching its first ready-to-wear collection of gender neutral wedding suits through BHLDN. It's not much of a departure since Bindle & Keep has already been making suits for individuals or couples headed for the altar. But it is the brand's first foray into ready-to-wear. Rae says, "We're implementing everything we've ever learned from making bespoke garments for our clients into making this dedicatedly inclusionary collection."

Towards the end of 2019, Daniel was deliberating the possibility of Bindle & Keep branching out of New York. He had been eyeing a commercial space in Philadelphia where they already had a growing base of loyal clients. Should things proceed according to plan, Philly may soon have its own top notch gender-neutral outfitter.

- - - - - - - -

A case can be laid out that Bindle & Keep, along with a host of other brands touting inclusive fashions, would not have ever existed pre-internet. The implacable changes wrought by the internet across all of known civilization are incalculable. True, social media has directed much needed attention to ongoing issues of prejudice, equality and equity, the rights of women, people of color, and the LGBTQ+ community. Unfortunately not all of these digital revolutions have been unquestionably benign. Within the fashion industry's convoluted network alone, not a single entity has been spared from the need to evolve, and do so fast, lest it perishes. Some of these evolutions have been particularly pernicious. The monthly glossy, for one, continues to suffer a brutally protracted form of impending demise - from reduced staffing to loss of ad revenues. No one can contest that the gathering and transfer of information have become more nimble, if not entirely efficiently fact-checked. But there are many who will profess that print magazines are already extinct. And that the only ones who don't know it yet are those working for them. But the reality is several fashion magazine titles are, much like Harris Tweed, priceless IPs and the print editions represent a level of eminence that can't ever be matched by a website. Face it, everyone and his cousin twice removed has one of those.

Some members of the press and wholesale buyers, meanwhile, have gradually retreated from runway shows, once the domain from which learned appraisals were made on what ends up being on magazine covers and department store floors six months down the line. Today, they have depreciated into hype-charged events open to anyone able to dispense callow, prosaic opinions to several thousand followers on social media. Some brands have even taken to showing online, the convenience of which then disabuses the average fashion editor from the need to be physically present. And since the public can stream those runway shows as well, frequently in real time, the expectation of being able to instantaneously buy what they see has created a new set of problems. A growing faction is responding to this with the arguably sensible call for adjusting to on-season production schedules. Many buyers, now so deathly terrified of gambling on something new, are already prone to buying for immediate deliveries and restocking what's obviously selling, anyway.

"In the US, specialty stores are disappearing," says Joseph Abboud. And he laments, "It's such a shame because it's often where someone has the latitude to take risks". He adds, "Retail would be so much different if there were more merchants who are, yes, 'financially responsible' while still being 'product, quality, and value-driven'." While he is sympathetic to how an uncertain economy has inured department store buyers into only placing "safe" orders, he is convinced this perpetuates the problem. "When the numbers drive the purchases, the selection suffers. And even if a buyer likes a new product, he may not be willing to stake his job on the probability that it may not sell."

From his end, Joseph refuses to compromise or become predictable. While, neither Joseph nor Paul Stuart's Ralph Auriemma have any plans of ever abandoning the Scottish mills for their quota of tweeds, they admittedly have nothing but praises for Italian mills such as Lanificio Egidio Ferla based in Biella with its novel approaches to the cloth. Founded in the 1800s by the grandfather of current head Paolo Ferla, the mill, says Joseph, "has always had a reputation for innovation and exceptional fabrics. When I first started working with them, their fabrics were simply far superior to what I had been used to seeing everywhere. They have a way of honoring English sensibility but giving it an Italian flavor." In other words, the Italians spin tweeds in new ways that celebrate British pomp without being constrained by the circumstance of arcane practices. And by concentrating on woolens instead of the worsted fabrics for which its region's other mills are popular, Ferla has become a leading go-to supplier of fashion forward tweeds.

Regardless of their manufacturing sources, Joseph is effusive about the original tweeds he's recently designed, featuring striking contrasts of darker shades such as charcoal and bursts of color such as rust. He holds up a swatch and smiles with some sage advice: "When everybody thinks they know where you are, be someplace else." Right about now, a good guess as to where Joseph might be headed would be somewhere elevated. Joseph Abboud Mountain, an all-new line created exclusively for the Japanese market came out for Autumn Winter 2019-2020. It's an apt name for a country composed of about three-quarters mountains and volcanoes. Before the launch, Joseph offered a hint that this new line sets sleek citified looks against a rustic backdrop, an approach similar to the Japanese propensity for a life best lived in accommodation of nature. And maybe more apropos of the function of these garments - trekking up mountain peaks or hiking and cycling around them are well-loved activities among both locals and tourists.

Joseph says he's excited to unveil the collection there since Japan is one of the few remaining markets in the world that "value creativity over middle-of-the-road sure sellers". And for a country that embraces the very latest in high tech thingamobobs, Japan still remains curiously resistant to making purchases via their phones, tablets or laptops. In Japan, small outfitters like Ethan Newton's Bryceland's and Firenze-based Liverano & Liverano are doing well with tweed garments, while record stores like HMV and Tower are still selling vinyl. Among business pundits, the prevailing theory is that for most local consumers, rifling through record bins or touching the garments are linchpins to having a gratifying shopping experience.

- - - - - - - - -

For London shoppers, a visit to Dashing Tweeds has become a one-stop tour of menswear options with the opening of other stores nearby like Grey Flannel, Trunk, bespoke tailor English Cut, Hamilton and Hare, and Casley-Hayford, which also has women's wear. And ever since Holly Pressdee joined the Dashing team as business director, the company has stepped up its operational aspects. She had the website set up, organized the collection roll outs, and managed many of the day-to-day business side of the brand. Dashing Tweeds has even set up its own made-to-measure services. Holly gives Guy and Kirsty more time envisioning how to ingeniously mix tweed with tech. By delving into how the natural aspect of their materials may be enhanced by cutting-edge concepts, Guy hopes to find more functional ways tweed can serve modern life. Guy says, "It's a balancing act. On one hand, we are becoming increasingly interested in working with single flock rare breed sheep to make highly desirable fabrics. And on the other, we are looking at experimenting with and potentially interpolating the very latest tech such as carbon nanotubes, graphene, etc. into tweed. I'd like Dashing to be a company wearable tech companies come to for creating luxurious 'smart clothing'."

- - - - - - - -

Although the Outer Hebrides may not be ready for the materials Guy has in mind, it is now more widely accepted that Alan Bain's push to make lighter weight tweeds was not as sacrilegious as was once thought. One year after it was shut down, the Kenneth McKenzie mill reopened and was relaunched by churning out lighter weight tweed jackets. In September 2019, its owner, Brian Haggas issued a startling announcement. He said he was retiring and handing over ownership of the mill to its production director Alex Lockerby. While no financial arrangement was disclosed, the handover was reported as a "gift". The magnanimous gesture, according to Haggas, was to prevent "financial vultures" from buying and stripping the company. In his official letter, he went on to say that the ownership and production of Harris Tweed belonged to the people of the Western Isles. Lockerby responded by saying he was "astounded by this act of generosity." The Harris Tweed saga of Brian Haggas ended on as abrupt a note as it had begun.

- - - - - - - -

Shetland, Donegal, and Harris tweeds comprise a great deal of Ralph Auriemma's latest collections for both his main Paul Stuart line and the "younger" Phineas Cole. A paean to the modern country gentleman, both collections boast unlined jackets and suits lacking canvas or shoulder pads but hold their shape by dint of excellent cuts and tailoring. Light and soft, they wear like cardigans but are no less splendid than a fully constructed garment. There are equestrian details and prints on fine wool, linen, and silk in varying weights sourced from English and Italian mills such as Loro Piana, Solbiati and Vitale Barberis to round out the collection. It will be rolled out once the renovations on the second floor of the flagship store are completed. There, Ralph has also reconfigured the areas offering the brand's recently-introduced customLAB made-to-measure services in full or half canvas constructions crafted by twenty onsite tailors.

As Ralph prepared to show these new collections, he began reminiscing of when he was still at Ralph Lauren. In 2003 when Purple Label held its first runway show in Milan, the team from New York encamped in the Italian city three weeks ahead to work out all the complicated logistics of getting a collection ready for showing. Interminable and arduous days were spent on the set, the lights, the seating, on assembling, fitting, and styling the clothes on the models. But they were no less exciting since Milan is deemed the epicenter of menswear showings. Lauren arrived a couple of days before the start of Milan Fashion Week and joined the staff for dinner at the brand's cafeteria. Ralph, who was seated at the end of a long communal table, found Lauren settling down directly across from him. Before he could take another bite of his food, Ralph suddenly noticed how his boss' patrician gaze had fallen upon him. And for the next few seconds, Ralph sat in anticipation of perhaps some instruction about the show. Instead, without warning, Lauren solemnly intoned, "Never stop dreaming." And Ralph says he never has.

- - - - - - - -

As for Lauren, he stepped down from his eponymous company in 2015 and relinquished his CEO duties to Stefan Larsson, the erstwhile global president of Old Navy. Two years later, Lauren took it back and ejected Larsson over the usual issues of "creative differences". In 2017, Patrice Louvet, former group president of global beauty brands at Proctor & Gamble, was appointed CEO and president, while Lauren remains as chief creative officer and chairman of the board.

Two years later, at the National Arts Club in New York, Lauren was the topic of one of its Fashion Fridays gatherings. The event is a season-long program of weekly get-togethers where club members and select fashion followers congregate to meet and hear fashion experts discuss certain aspects of their crafts. On this particular evening, Alan Flusser sat before a rapt crowd in the second floor gallery of the club's Gramercy Park headquarters to talk about his new book "Ralph Lauren: In His Own Fashion". Alan had spent twelve years putting together the heavily illustrated, 304-page biography. For his appearance, Alan wore a suit of the same tartan pattern that he had chosen as the book cover. Dubbed the "definitive" book on Lauren and made with his full cooperation, the tome benefited from Alan's unrestricted access to Lauren's archives and to countless of their industry contemporaries. On why he had dedicated years to the project, Alan the inveterate perfectionist says he was only willing to let it go to print after it was completed to his utter satisfaction.

- - - - - - - -

Lore, fortified by time, may be viewed as tweed's strength and weakness. For that very reason, tweed becomes more seductive a medium for designers to ceaselessly re-examine, dismantle then reassemble, tweak, repurpose or altogether re-imagine. And many have given it their best shot. In 2003, the oft-copied Miuccia Prada unveiled her Fall men's and women's collections, both featuring tweed coats and fedoras. There were houndstooth tweed handbags and pumps as well. Implying calculated disarray, one short, unbuttoned tweed coat was worn over a black mini dress and off-handedly cinched with a thin brown belt. And nothing in either her supremely intellectual collections betrayed so much as a soupçon of nostalgia. In fact, that season, Prada debuted a new cut for its coats with yoke shoulders and funnel necklines that fall narrowly below the clavicle.

The following year saw Jean-Paul Gaultier taking over the reins of Hermès with tweed coats and roomy trousers on show at the École Militaire cavalry training ground. Observers sitting amidst bales of hay were delighted by the designer's respectful treatment of the Parisian brand's classic equestrian themes while injecting them with Gaultieresque touches. Then there's Japanese designer Junya Watanabe, who began his career as patternmaker at Comme des Garçons, and has since built a solo brand with collections that prod menswear beyond clichés. That ubiquitous Levi's denim jacket? He's made one in tweed. He's collaged materials together in one item no one else could've imagined. Moleskin and cotton? Check. Wool and denim? Check. A single breasted coat of neoprene-bonded tweed with black synthetic leather sleeves? Check and check. Watanabe-san's deft manipulations of tweed are simply without bounds.

At Chanel, Virginie Viard took over as creative director of the house after Herr Lagerfeld died in 2019. Her 2020 couture collection is rumored to be introducing a glittering new way of combining a couple of the brand's staples - tweed and bold accessories - for a jewelry line called Tweed de Chanel. Details are sparse but what's sure is Linton Tweeds is, alas, not involved. An early press photo showed what the brand is calling a "Tweed Graphique" bracelet, an 18-ct white gold, onyx and diamond marvel set in an intersecting tweed-like pattern. And tweed's future is looking bright indeed.

The fundamentally fleeting nature of fashion is why its aesthetics are often most clearly discerned in the ephemera of what industry professionals routinely refer to as "a moment". The conversion of the noun from common to proper has found other colloquial uses. But in fashion, it's a lightning-in-a-bottle collision of the right garment, on the right person, in the right setting, with the right atmosphere, and perhaps accompanied by the right music – a visual and wearable idiom raised to its apotheosis. When it strikes, it does so as both a sublime experience and an inspiration. Hence the ceaseless pursuit of the next such moment. It is the stuff of dreams, captured and immortalized in photographs or film, tacked onto mood boards, designed into collections, sought out at runway shows or on red carpets, lovingly remembered, referenced, and subsequently recreated or re-invented. Of course now, the cavalcade of social media feeds programmed to lure and elicit populist approval have taken to preserving these images for posterity though mostly divested of chronological context.

True, the same may be said of tweed's capability to persist past seasons, past lifetimes, and therefore in contradiction to fashion's temporal ideals. Time and again, tweed could very easily have slipped away into irrelevance, were it not for the intervention of people committed to its unwavering charm and limitless uses. It is tweed's temperament of ineffable erudition that has led each generation to seek aspects of the cloth to make their very own, in hopes of discovering new moments. Discourses on the subject are and will be ceaseless. And those tales will continue to be told, traveling as tales do from garment to wearer, from fathers to sons, from designers to artisans, from culture to culture. But no matter the plot twists, one thing may be agreed upon by those kindred spirits who live, breathe, design, study, weave, craft, sell, buy, understand, appreciate, or just enjoy wearing fine clothes: tweed truly is where the heart is.

One fine Spring day in 2018, Will got the call from Andrew at long last. Five weeks after work on the suit started, it was ready. All the months of planning and anticipation had culminated into the elation of putting on the three-piece tweed suit with its "swelled chest, suppressed waist, and full-cut trousers". Will says with typical British understatement, "It was wonderful seeing it completed and then finally being able to put it on. The fit was amazing. And I was so pleased with the details and how it had been executed, especially the trousers with the high waistband and wide leg." Not too long after, Will took the suit out for a spin, so to speak. "I went for a bike ride in the suit and it was perfect!" he enthuses. But because they had left the trousers unlined, he laughingly admits, "They were just a bit scratchy 'round the legs where the cloth was rubbing me! But, at cycling speed, the tweed does let in a refreshingly cooling breeze." Will should get good use of the suit at informal gatherings in the city or the country. It would also be the thing to wear whenever he joins Andrew's annual informal tweed ride with close friends in the Fall. And for Will nothing beats wearing his best tweeds for a bike ride out into the rapturous, tangerine glow of a New York sunset.

Acknowledgments

For so generously sharing their invaluable time and experience, or in a variety of other ways aided and abetted in the making of this book, my sincerest gratitude goes to:

Will Burghes+ Guy Hills + Alan L. Bain + Patrick Grant + Ralph Auriemma + Alan Flusser + Andrew Yamato + Joseph Abboud + Bill Rancitelli + John Bartlett + Nicholas Hammond + Sigrid Tate Gouze + Shaun Leane + Heather Bain + Jane Greenwood + John David Ridge + Victoria Christie + Peter Sandel + Tracy Christensen + Noll Uloth + W. David Marx + Kirsty McDougall + Keith Walker + Catherine Aitken + Rosy Temple + Daniel Friedman + Rae Tutera + Oliver Mak + Adam Glant + Martin Hunt + Joy Buensalido + John Morgan + Lisa Wertheimer Wells + Peter Cruz + Michael Stefanov + Matt Zaremba + Ann Hould-Ward + Stephen A. Garner + Olivia Gillespie-Norris + Marion Mulhern + Hillary Becque + Lusmila McColl + Jonathan Sloth-Nielsen + Edward P. Turco + Stephen McCahill + Brian Herron + Edward M. Bradley + Janet Glover + Tommy Boudreau + Gina Gibbons + Lucy May + Jonathan Sigmon + Holly Pressdee + Steven M. Gillon + Christopher Blomquist + Sandra Nygaard + Stefan Steil + Keith Sherman + Jodi Cornish + Susan Deiters + Scott Klein + Joven Relova + Dorothy Mannfolk + Angel Rivera+ Jona McClenning + Mark McClenning + and my entire family